You Have the Right to Remain Silent

You Have the Right to Remain Silent

Bringing
Meditation to Life

RICK LEWIS

Hohm Press
Prescott, Azizona

Cover design: Kim Johansen
Layout and design: Bookworks, San Diego, California

Library of Congress Cataloging-in-Publication-Data:

Lewis, Rick, 1961–
You have the right to remain silent: bringing meditation to life / Rick Lewis
    p. cm.
Includes biblographical references and index.
    ISBN 1-890772-23-2 (pbk. : alk. paper)
1. Meditation. I. Title.
BL627.L495 2002
291.4'35—dc21

                                           2002006640

Hohm Press
P.O. Box 2501,
Prescott, AZ 86302
800-381-2700
http://www.hohmpress.com

This book was printed in the U.S.A. on
acid-free paper using soy ink.

06 05 04 03 02   4 3 2 1

To the earth for something to sit on.
To my parents for something to observe.
To Lee for Observation itself.

Contents

The Wild Heart of Silence

Preface

What meditation is in all traditions, faiths and forms is virtually unlimited. There are the mantra, visualization, contemplation, asanas, chanting, deity worship, active meditation, art, whirling, sex, and the praying that we do when we go to the dentist, just off the top of my head. While this book is indeed meant to be a serious look at the practice of meditation, there are many types of meditative practices which I am simply unable to address here.

The purpose of this book is to share my own experience of *sitting meditation* and to make that experience relevant and understandable to Westerners of any faith. You do not have to believe any dogma or buy any prepackaged convictions to benefit from sitting practice or the contents of this book.

I can't tell you exactly where meditation in the form of sitting practice originated. We do know, however, that it was a heck of a long time ago, in the East somewhere, way past New Jersey, and that it has probably been practiced in fundamentally the same manner for many thousands of years. The point of sitting practice is that we come to know where meditation originates in *us*, and that is the focus of this book.

I speak in this book about my own spiritual school without naming it in the text. Just for the record, it is called the Western Baul tradition. My own practice is steeped in the influence of that tradition and its founder, spiritual master Khépa Lee Baul, also known as Lee Lozowick, who actually *is* from New Jersey.

My teacher demonstrates an unusually vast appreciation and working knowledge of spiritual traditions, literature and masters, consistent with the wide borrowing tendencies of the original Bauls of the East. It is due to his broad regard for practice in its many forms that individuals such as Chögyam Trungpa Rinpoche, Arnaud Desjardins, Taisen Deshimaru, Suzuki Roshi and Werner Erhard have made their way into my own heart and subsequently into this book. Even so, I primarily draw upon my own teacher for guidance and inspiration, and that is reflected here. I am reminded of a comment I heard Paul Newman make many years ago about his wife, Joanne Woodward, when he was asked how he kept himself out of the tabloids. He said something to the effect of, "Why would I go out to eat when I have steak at home?" I do not expect anyone else to agree with or adopt my own, obviously defined, orientation, but only to tolerate it as the natural result of my personal circumstance.

Finally, let's keep in mind that if we (meaning you, the reader, and me, the writer) want you (meaning you) to get anything out of this book, we're going to have to make a collaborative effort. I am the world's leading expert in my own point of view, as you are in yours, so let's not let that get in our way, shall we?

Introduction

I am a man in his early forties and the father of two children, one of whom is still young enough to be on my lap at this very moment, thinking that it's really cool the way this computer writes things.

There—enough about me. Why don't you tell me something about yourself? I'd like to know to whom I'm speaking so I can tailor my material to suit your particular interests, likes, dislikes, dreams and hopes. Ready? Go. (You speak for one-tenth of a second here and then we move on.)

I'm just getting you warmed up—preparing you for how much life, in the form of reality, gives a hoot about my or your agendas, preferences and "personal" needs ~~~ and if we're going to try the practice of meditation, that's what we're going to find out.

Life itself, *as it is*, does not take into account what we *think* life should be like when it wakes us up in the morning, ~~~~ or how we think others should treat us—what kind of acknowledgement we should get for our talents, skills, abilities and sacrifices. ~~

As an example, in this exact moment my four-year-old wants to press buttons. All those misplaced squiggly symbols are hers. What *I'm* wanting to do in this moment is just write my heart out, but she is curious and asking lots of questions and has three hundred and thirty-seven fingers, all of which want to touch everything in the universe. So here I am, caught between the life I *imagine* I am here to live in this moment—and what is actually being called of me to embrace.

And if you think that three hundred and thirty-seven fingers is an exaggeration, then you probably don't have children, or weren't one yourself for some bizarre reason that we can't imagine. I was once in a restaurant with my family when our server, who was obviously a parent himself, asked my wife and me if we knew how to calculate what a child can reach. When we said no, which was apparent due to the fact that everything on the table had been turned upside-down, broken, dropped or licked, he said, "You measure the length of the child's arm and multiply by four."

That particular equation pretty much translates right across the board to the untrained mind. Its reach surprises us and boggles us not infrequently, and that which it reaches almost always gets turned upside-down, toppled from a stable and innocent condition, and is left in some form of disrepair or disarray, leaving us with sudden reason for concern. Why do children and the mind have to do that?

So what does "you have the right to remain silent" mean? How can we use words to communicate the essence of silence? How does one speak of an invisible gem, a weightless gold that by its very nature defies any type of description?

Poets and fools try. A few lines from Shakespeare's Twenty-seventh Sonnet come close.

> Save that my soul's imaginary sight
> Presents thy shadow to my sightless view,
> Which like a jewel (hung in ghastly night)
> Makes black night beauteous, and her old face new.

Fortunately, this book is not an attempt to communicate silence itself. It is rather intended to offer a method of becoming *vulnerable to the experience* of silence in our lives.

I'd like nothing more than uninterrupted writing time right now. My daughter's preschool, however, is closed for the holidays. We've made an agreement that we can play some, but then Dad also has to work some—"and you can play quietly," I explain.

"Okay," she agrees.

She is now sitting right next to me, and "playing quietly" at this exact moment looks like counting each and every one of the keys on the computer keyboard, inches away. The question is, am I going to have a "thing" about it; dwell on the wish that her school's holiday schedule even came close to acknowledging the reality of parenting, and secretly harbor resentment that I'm having to split my attention instead of being able to focus on my writing? Will I feel compelled to yank on the thin, loose thread that dangles out of my head in such moments—a thread of thought which when pulled recites the phrase, "Why me?" From my experience I know that to pull on that thread is to unravel the whole garment of my relationship to life-as-it-is. Still, I often tear at those threads, even when I know better.

Silence reigns when there is no commentary shadowing the flow of life as it presents itself to us. We either act in response to what arises or we confront the moment with our naked composure; confront it not in opposition, but in willingness to be "face to face" with that moment.

"Dad, can I do another squiggly line?"

"No, that's enough squiggly lines right now."

The phrase "you have the right to remain silent" is, of course, most often delivered by a law enforcement officer as a warning to an individual who is charged with a crime. The warning is a reminder to that person that their words could implicate them in a serious offense. For the meditator, the phrase is a reminder that our thoughts may implicate us in a serious swamp of commentary.

Commentary comes in many forms and could appear to be negative or positive. It comes as value judgment: "This is good," or "This is bad"; as degrees of satisfaction: "This is enough," or "This is not enough"; as pride or blame: "I did this," or "You did that." Commentary, however, acknowledges only one hand of an ambidextrous universe, which leaves us unable to hold life-as-it-is. We need both hands for that.

When we see life-as-it-is, we share its wholeness. To see life-as-it-is is to step out of the commentator's box, which automatically reveals the "basic goodness" of our true nature, as the Tibetan Buddhist meditation master Chögyam Trungpa Rinpoche has called it. Acceptance, elegance, delight, clarity, and spaciousness all arise in our recognition of a world which is not divided, but complete.

So the right to remain silent is not a license for withdrawal. Nor does it correspond to the nonuse of our voice in daily life. The right to remain silent describes the potential we have to fully embrace our current condition, both internally and externally, without apology, justification, and confusion, but with grace, integrity, and perpetual uprightness.

With practice, silence can become our internal orientation

even when we are passionately active in our world. Silence is the result of bringing meditation to life. In the initial stages of our practice, however, we are bound to bring our life into meditation. Out of habit, we clutter the openings into which our minds could be expanding and treat the natural spaciousness of awareness like a landfill, as a dumping ground for the excess produced by our industrial-strength commentary: the mass production of shoulds, what-ifs, how-comes, when-wills, fantasies, anxieties, and desires.

When we drag our lives into meditation we may fail to notice, even for days or weeks, that when we sit in formal meditation we are actually sitting right on top of the possibility for this profound silence. There may be no gap between the closing of our eyes and the projection of our mental busyness onto the screen of awareness. Or we may bring our lives even literally into the meditation environment—entering a sacred space which has been designed as a refuge from the mundane with a cell phone in our pocket or with a trail of cigarette smoke on our coattails.

The right to remain silent is the right to shift our perspective from the chatter in our head down into the body. When we descend into our bodies through meditation, we break the surface of reason and contemplation. We are even now standing neck deep, immersed in an ocean of delight, wonder and blessings—yet if we are living only in the head, we will miss the fact that the body is already drenched in truth, the baptism already consummated.

Even though we have a purpose here, that purpose goes far beyond reason; extends far beyond the realm of explanations, theories and intellectual cosmologies. It is when that purpose is *felt,* through and through, that we know we have come upon the silent place within us.

What is Meditation?

CHAPTER ONE

A Guide for the West of Us

Understanding Is the Booby Prize

Off we go! Isn't this exciting? But before we lift off, there are a few bases we need to cover. Perhaps you are a novice meditator, interested in beginning a practice of meditation but wanting some practical support to get started. You may be looking for something to inspire you to begin a sitting practice, or you may already have a meditation practice and would like to deepen it, or confirm what you already know. Perhaps you are in some kind of pain and seek relief from your condition.

This is all well and good, although I am required to inform you that you are currently in danger; in danger of becoming not inspired, but discouraged. The material in this first section may not be the news we want to hear. Most of us want to hear how well we are doing, and how meditation will give us peace, happiness, contentment and insight. Indeed, it eventually does that—and more. However, the initial stages of a meditation practice are the initial stages of waking up from a dream life—a life in which we are not required to make efforts, not required to feel confusion and anguish, not required to face facts.

Irina Tweedie, lineage holder to Bhai Sahib in the Sufi tradition and author of the spiritual classic *Daughter of Fire,* was delivering a lecture on spiritual transformation and sharing stories of her practice and her life with her teacher. After she had communicated some of the agony and torment she faced prior to her own breakthrough, a young man in the audience raised his hand and asked, "Isn't there some way we can walk this path without all the difficulty, the suffering and the pain?" Mrs. Tweedie looked up at him with utmost tenderness and answered, "I'm afraid not, young man."

The demand of practice does not lift us up, but takes us down and through. It does not initially inspire us, but causes first the expiration of old approaches, makes them lifeless and untenable. It is entirely possible that you might experience uncomfortable feelings as you read, but it's crucial to understand that this discomfort and any discouragement that might arise is a very good sign, and unavoidable in establishing a foundation for real meditation. You may want to debate or disagree with what you're reading, but don't let that stop you from continuing. Let the discouragement happen; let your current edifice of understanding crumble. Werner Erhard, founder of the EST program and later the Landmark Forum, has said, "Understanding is the booby prize."

Understanding is the booby prize because understanding changes nothing. An old Zen master once told his disciple, "If you are wrong, I give you thirty blows and if you are right . . . I give you thirty blows." Whether we are wrong or right, understanding this way or that, doesn't matter. Giving up the booby prize will make our progress much easier, though it won't feel comfortable or secure. We will much sooner begin to appreciate the beauty and value of bare land, though we may for a while grieve our castle of ideas about life, meditation, spirituality and being human.

Being with Ourselves as We Are

The conditioning of our early childhood has programmed us with a limited range of responses to life situations, and our ability to respond to our current adult circumstances is seriously handicapped by these early adopted strategies for getting love and attention. Instead of interacting with our world based on a true view of what is before us, we relate to it through the filter of our past.

Though we may agree intellectually with that analysis, most of us don't know this to be true; we haven't *seen* it, since the beliefs, attitudes and biases on which we base our behavior are virtually invisible to us. Nor are these attitudes stamped only on our minds.

Many years ago I enrolled in a liberal and very intensive program of development for actors which revolved around a professional theater conservatory. In order to be able to represent the life of a character on stage we were trained first in "neutrality"—how to rid ourselves of predominating traits or characteristics so that when it came time to build a character, that character was not contaminated with our own personal patterns and habits. The entire first year of this four-year training program was dedicated to this process of deconstructing the prominent characteristics of our personas, especially with respect to our speech patterns, emotional patterns and body postures.

One class involved mask work in which we took turns wearing a black body suit and an opaque white plastic mask over our face in front of the group. The mask was completely neutral in expression, displaying no particular feeling or emotion, but when it was worn by each individual it began to communicate a tremendous range of attitude, even though our clothing was uncharacteristic and our body posture as neutral as we could make it. Worn by one student the mask was angry, for another sad, for another flirtatious, then unmistakably defiant, and so on. We had no idea to what extent we carried these unconscious attitudes as the default expression of our bodies in our ordinary waking lives.

Spiritual practice and meditation is about beginning to get inside of that process, realize that it's going on, and see that our biases, our behavior, our actions, our speech, our thoughts have all been conditioned. Instead of simply observing the external manifestations of our world and then leaping into action, we learn to direct our attention toward our interior reality as well and consider the process by which we apply interpretation and judgment to our perceptions. Only when we can reliably bring this double-edged, well-sharpened type of attention to the process of observing the "truth" can we consider serving what is real instead of being locked into our preconceived notion of "what is." Meditation gives us the ability to be with things as they are and respond to them appropriately.

It requires tremendous vigilance, understanding, education and courage to purge and purify the unconscious elements that are involved in our perceptions of reality. Most of what is being offered under the guise of "spirituality" in the West—quick fixes promising to alleviate pain and confusion and suffering—are only causing deeper pain and confusion and suffering. Not because our suffering is not addressable, but because the suffering we undergo is being enacted in the basements of our own houses, in the torture chambers of our own unconscious. That which appears to be remedial only perpetuates our suffering because the remedy is ignorant of the illusions that are held by those it intends to cure. Unfortunately, in some cases those who are selling such fixes have actually taken the illusions of their buying public into account and are exploiting that public by bringing products to market which will appeal precisely to those with particular blind spots.

Take, for example, a recent television commercial for a new truck which sports the campaign slogan, "To be one with everything, you've got to have one of everything." Some advertising ploys, like this one, appear as blatant attempts to appeal to our baser nature, while others are much more sly and subtle. The overall effect, however, of our being bombarded by the promotion of product is devastating. In an article called "Zen Sells," author Todd Stein reports,

> By the time the average American reaches twenty, they will have seen about one million TV commercials. Those numbers add up to an undeniable truth; they have been programmed since childhood to seek fulfillment through buying.[1]

Eager for relief from our pain, we spiritual shoppers lunge at anything which is shrink-wrapped and sports any combination of the words "organic," "natural," or "healing" on the label. These panaceas are not going to fix anything, because the real fix is a very painstaking process. As H. L. Mencken once said, "For every human problem, there is a neat, simple solution; and it is always wrong." I think that pretty well sums up our situation as far as much of spirituality in the West is concerned.

Even though there are all sorts of practices, mantras, visualizations and techniques which we are now getting our hands on via Easterners who are coming to the West to "teach," through books or even through the Internet, those fragments were originally delivered in the context of an entire tradition that included many other elements that we aren't privy to in the process of shopping the way we shop in the West and acquiring spiritual technology. In San Jose, California, just near the San Jose airport there is a street called Technology Drive. In America technology has become a destination, a place. It is now an end in itself, no longer a means to an end.

I was recently in a health club and standing next to a treadmill where a woman was just finishing her exercise period. As she climbed down off of the machine, a friend came up and embraced her and asked, "How was your run?" Though the woman did get "exercise"—elevate her heart rate and strengthen muscles—the assumption that she had "run" struck me as being out of place. What if actually breathing fresh outdoor air, having to watch one's footfall, making decisions in the moment about where to run, moderating one's own speed and pace, and learning to negotiate hills both physically and psychologically, to give just a few examples, are all essential features of what makes up running? Was she getting the benefit that nature intends from our modified, contrived and convenient version of "running"? It's debatable. The point is that we are getting used to our ability to pull things out of context as a culture and isolate products, benefits and systems. Yet we are doing so without a sufficient knowledge of context—we do not have a broad enough view to see the importance of the relationships which surround the objects we are attempting to value. This is especially true in our pursuit of healing and growth in the areas of health and spirituality. We will talk more later about the importance of context with respect to spiritual practice.

There are fewer and fewer cultures in existence which have at their root any recognition of or appreciation for the fact that resting in reality as it is has value, meaning and importance. Most cultures are replacing the rituals, practices and spiritually affirming roots that may have been developed or handed down over generations with variations of neurosis that are built upon mankind's now technologically aided capability to control, dominate and manage reality according to its own whims.

We justify all this activity by pretending that we are "evolving" and things are changing. But what underlies the entire technological movement and the domination of our environment is our own fear of transformation itself. This can be clearly observed by studying our relationship to even our own modern day myths, such as the Superman story, which is essentially interesting to us because it represents the transformational process. In the Superman myth it used to be that our hero, in response to the need of others, would enter into an ordinary phone booth and emerge transformed, endowed with the powers he required to meet the needs of the suffering.

Today's media darlings and heroes, by contrast, are those who enter the phone booth and transform not themselves, but the phone booth. The "hero" emerges completely unchanged, yet becomes a multimillionaire or billionaire overnight.

One of my children came home after school one day and said, "Daddy, I know a quick way to count to one hundred."

"How?" I asked.

"One, two . . . skip a few . . . ninety-nine, one hundred!"
Our relationship to practice in the West is unfortunately
reflected in this type of shortcutting. As Ken Wilber puts it in
his book, *A Brief History of Everything,*

> We prefer a "spirituality" that takes whatever level we
> are at and gives us a "one-step" process that will get us
> straight to God, instantly, like a microwave oven. We
> deny stages altogether and end up with a very flatland
> notion.[2]

A great deal of what is happening in our culture is the opposite of what is necessary to make human beings fertile soil
for true spiritual practice, mature enough to be able to be a
host to this thing called "grace." Our technology downplays
the necessity of human relationship and human contact, including the need for real living teachers as role models. Our
economic system encourages excess in all ways and lacks
compassion for those who are disadvantaged within it. Our
education system is completely ill-equipped to transmit
principles of right living and spiritual knowledge. In most
ways we're distancing ourselves from the basic wisdom of
the body through the use of our advancements and artificial
creations, everything from all the supplements which are fu-
eling the gigantic growth of the health food industry, to ge-
netically modified food, to digital "reality." And this is all
based on our desperate desire to escape our pain and suffering without addressing the root causes of it.

We want so desperately to "understand" our condition,
to have someone explain it to us. But in transforming our
understanding we are in no way guaranteed the transformation of *ourselves.* Long ago we transformed our understanding of nicotine without transforming our relationship, as

individuals or as a culture, to addiction. Transformation is scary and risky business because we can never enjoy it: the one who wants to be transformed disappears if his wish comes true. This has always been a dilemma for human beings.

With our minds we look at the chamber of transformation from the outside and, describing the externally visible features of it in great detail, try and convince ourselves that we're now liberated by our new understanding. But we aren't and we know it; we feel it. And we never will be truly liberated from our untransformed condition until we walk into the chamber itself, go the distance within, and are reordered by the transformational power of its pressure. Yes, we can get in touch with and be graced by certain types of revelation or insight—inspired or grazed by what really is a spiritual influence—but in order to be able to hold what we get touched by and sustain it, and live our lives on the basis of it, we have to train our mind and body in a way that makes them continually vulnerable and receptive to that influence. Again, we have to address the root cause of our pain.

The root cause is our inability to be with ourselves as we are. There's an old saying which says that if you're in prison and you want to get out, the first thing you need to do is admit that you're in prison. We're under the profound misconception in Western culture that we're free. We believe without pause in the reality of our freedom, and we routinely defend that belief with both rhetoric and the practice of our "right to bear arms." In actuality, we are simply in a prison from which we get to choose between several different types of cookies for dessert; between these jeans that we can scarcely breathe in or those jeans that we can scarcely breathe in. The provision of choice, or "options," is intentional upon the part of the imprisoning agent; it gives us the illusion that we have autonomy, individuality and freedom.

When we begin to investigate the unconscious conditioning which we all carry around, however, we begin to realize that we're simply mechanical. Something happens and it's like a button has been pushed: "A" stimulus creates "B" response in us. The dollars spent by Madison Avenue researching the predictability of those buttons, and the additional expenditure to systematically design advertising which takes advantage of our mechanical nature, bear it out.

There is nothing we protect so fiercely as our beliefs, and there is nothing we leave so undefended and unmanaged as our attention. It's like owning a priceless computer, unparalleled in speed, agility and power, yet allowing anyone and everyone to log on and bang into us their own programming. In this culture, in this age, there is one thing of which we can be sure—our beliefs are not "ours"; our preferences, our tastes, our opinions are all programming which someone or something with an interest in its own perpetuation has downloaded into our database at some point in the history of our pure, undefended and vulnerable mind.

Becoming free has to do with seeing ourselves as we are, seeing that we act more like machines than individuals, and that can be an extremely painful process. It's very difficult to really observe ourselves as we are and realize that the behavior we have always rationalized or justified as appropriate is simply the face of our own cruelty, pride, self-love or apathy; or to admit that we use food to avoid our feelings, or that we're so caught up in our own mind that we're not even really present in our relationships.

Ours is not a culture that is comfortable with human feeling. Remorse, sadness, anger, passion naturally arise by virtue of simply being human, yet we have all these layers that are piled on top of simple humanness; injunctions against human experience and feeling. Living out these injunctions has become an invisible process. We think we're just doing normal North American life, and we are, but we've been sold a belief that this "norm" is healthy, progressive and right, when actually it's deadly to our evolution and growth, both as individuals and as a culture, because we won't risk seeing how we *are*, and so we cannot move on.

Real meditation is a profanity as far as the self-improvement movement and the New Age are concerned. It is not for our personal benefit, though there may be side effects to a meditation practice that we consider to be personally preferable. Its essential function in God's plan is not to make us healthier, stress free, more attractive to the opposite sex, wealthier or happier. The practice of meditation, both formal and informal, is not for the purpose of spiffing ourselves up, becoming more holy, composed or adorable. Nor is it a means of renovating our personality, adding a new wing onto our dream image so that we can have more elbow room and larger mirrors in which to reflect upon ourselves.

Meditation is rather a deconstruction, the unbuffering of all the lies which we have been told and which we tell ourselves. Some of those lies are mild—practically harmless— and others are accomplices to terrible conspiracies that serve our separation from others.

The essential function of meditation is to become reliably available to what evolution itself wants in each moment. To sit, to open to what we truly are, strikes at all that we as a predominantly materialistic and "progressive" culture hold sacred. There is a kind of reverence we have for all those things that protect the prisons in which we hold our awareness.

If that reverence, which is really a self-love, a dream we do not want disturbed, gets shaken, we start arguing and defending and justifying ourselves.

We go to our teacher, our doctor, minister or friend with tears in our eyes and an old bone in our mouths. "How can I get rid of this thing?" we implore them. And then, when they suggest that we just drop the old thing, we growl, bare our teeth, run away and bury the toxic relic in a safe place in our backyard where we know we'll be able to find it if things get too good.

Yes, I really meant to say "too good." We are habituated to a level of energy, joy, brightness, clarity and strength which is like a trickle from a kinked-up garden hose, and any more than that scares the hell out of us. We say we want joy, clarity, power and love, but when we truly open to ourselves as we are and make ourselves vulnerable to all of life, we get a flow the force of Niagara Falls as a result and have no idea how to handle it. So we block it off, shut it down, overeat, numb out in our own special ways in order to keep ourselves "safe" from that kind of vitality, which is threatening to our sense of self, to who we have always been, or tried to be.

Initially, the meditative life is a process of backtracking; reversing the pattern we've been weaving until now. Instead of becoming further entangled in the fabric of life, we take the sharp point of our attention and turn it back on ourselves, on exactly the point where we last entered the world, and we push back through that fabric, freeing ourselves of at least that entanglement. Then we follow that thread further, and by moving back precisely through every last entry point, every attachment, we slowly loose ourselves from the mundane, until eventually we are completely unfettered. Once we know how to do this—how to fall back into ourselves and unwind the knots that hold us down in unwanted patterns—we are free to weave as we wish, in any way that is needed, because we always know how to extricate ourselves when the thread becomes binding, when it hinders the wishes of our heart.

We do this by being with ourselves as we are. Not as we are in theory, in concept, in self-image, but as we are in *life*. The way our thighs flatten out when we sit down, the way our back aches in the morning, the tenderness that sweeps over us when we witness the innocence of our children, the way we don't want to stop when lovemaking has naturally come to an end, the happiness we feel when called by a friend, the criticisms we level without thinking of what it costs the recipient.

So that's the task. To develop the strength to be with ourselves as we are so we can begin to be honest about the pain we're causing ourselves and others through our behavior; through our denials and what it is that we're running from. And also to start to admit the nearly unbearable goodness that besieges us in simple moments and not to give such treasure away so cheaply in the next, but to nurture it as seed for our practice. These are the first steps.

Participation in Life–As–It–Is

Meditation represents the appropriateness and necessity of participating in life-as-it-is; of active participation in our own Western culture; of embracing the ordinary activities which define basic human sanity, relationship and enterprise: right livelihood; responsibility to our parents and family members; the practice of kindness, generosity and compassion; and basic integrity in the world.

Unfortunately, many aspirants seek a spiritual path as a means of escaping from the basic responsibilities and demands which ordinary human life brings. Consequently, many spiritual movements in the West attempt to bypass this first and most fundamental requirement on the path of transformation. This attempted skirting of life itself at its most ordinary, material and human level short-circuits the possibility of engaging our transformational potential.

This is so because it is in and through the basic strengthening of ego itself that human consciousness can receive the transmission of knowledge ultimately sought on the path. The very ego whose nature it is to want, to desire, to define goals and move toward them, is the force that propels human consciousness into the territory that can deliver ultimate understanding. Naturally endowed with a mandate that orients it toward achievement, accomplishment, and material or social gain, ego is set in motion in a way that exposes it to a wide variety of phenomena in the world. Ego prompts the activity of the body and mind, and the body/mind is the carrier agent of consciousness; therefore, as ego is engaged, consciousness is subjected to the same broad range of influences and impressions.

It is the lure of reward for ego itself that causes ego to act, to participate. If ego participates, then, to a greater or lesser degree depending upon the individual, consciousness participates. The foundational premise of true meditation is not to limit the activities of ego, but rather to allow these activities and then to assert the presence of conscious awareness in tandem with them. It is only this alchemy between our presence and our participation in ordinary life that has the power to awaken the transformational process. Eventually, ego's predominating perspective is subsumed in the context of meditative life, but, paradoxically, this stage cannot reliably stand on the shoulders of a weak ego.

CHAPTER TWO

The Art of Staying Home

By age fifteen I found myself to be a typically "Type A" personality, driven to succeed in as many areas as I could juggle at once and convinced that only perfect success would afford me the acknowledgement, love and admiration I craved. I was busy every day after school with my own practices, most of which were athletic pursuits, and in the evenings with involvement in theater productions. My life was quite literally centered around my "performance," either on a playing field or on stage.

I remember one day, after arriving home from school, having my parents tell me that they would be out for the evening. As it so happened, my younger brother also had plans to be away from home. I can still recall the panic I felt when the realization hit me that I myself had no plans and would be home alone. There was always the television as a distraction, and I had a list of things I could have dedicated myself toward accomplishing, but I felt a sudden pang of concern for my own state of mind and the lack of ease in my body. I saw the fierce anxiety that I held underneath the surface of all of my activity, felt the knot in my own gut, and recognized that it couldn't be a good thing.

I made a decision in that moment that after everyone left the house that evening I would sit on the couch for thirty minutes and do nothing, just to prove that I could sit still for that long and be with myself without a task, goal or distraction. I wasn't at all sure that I was capable of this feat, but felt the necessity of making the attempt.

Predictably, it was very difficult. My mind raced from thought to thought; desires, fantasies and intense fears began surfacing with a vengeance; and I sweated out the thirty long minutes shifting back and forth uncomfortably. My mind tried to convince me that this little "exercise" was pointless, unnecessary, and that I would be much better served engaging in an activity that had meaning and clear purpose. But I stayed on the couch that night and since then have never ceased to value and practice the art of "staying home."

The journey we must make to wind through the labyrinth of our conditioning and find our own deep inner silence is full of paradoxes and contradictions. While we must want to reach the goal with all our heart, we must simultaneously resist the temptation to go off in search of it, since, in an inexplicable and strange way, we already possess what we are longing to attain, though we may feel distanced from it.

One of the most common errors we Western spiritual dilettantes make is to attempt to take on responsibility for things which are completely beyond the domain of human control while correspondingly abdicating responsibility for the only areas in which we can make a difference. We seem

anxious to claim responsibility for our "soul" through all
sorts of belief systems, hopes, affirmations and spiritual distractions, all the while ignoring some crucial basics.

Ninety-nine Percent

Ninety-nine percent of success or progress on a spiritual
path is due to miracles, magic and grace; ninety-nine percent of movement on the path occurs by virtue of a force that
is beyond our control. That leaves one percent, obviously, and
the one percent that is left is the part that we are responsible
for as a meditator or practitioner. It's only one percent of the
whole ball of wax, but it is a huge responsibility, a gigantic
undertaking; a responsibility few will accept. It requires
tremendous vigilance, intention, persistence and necessity to
handle this one percent, which we might call the domain of
practice or right living, at the center of which are the principles of meditation, or the art of staying home.

Let us not console ourselves with anything less than the
understanding that to achieve a right life, rooted in the practice of presence, is a lot of work. The other ninety-nine percent of the path, which is accomplished for us, will one day
become our great blessing and joy. But we cannot benefit
from this ninety-nine percent—this ninety-nine percent
cannot lawfully put itself into play—unless we do the work
of the one percent.

We need to understand some basic things about the nature
of our humanness at a psychological level before we can even
begin to be responsible for this tiny one percent of work that
is ours. The first thing we need to come to grips with is the reality of the fact that we do not have a relationship to ourselves,
which is the entire basis of the ability to remain home.

We do not have a relationship to ourselves because of the

betrayal we experienced in the hands of our parents or caretakers. In a perfect world, we would have received, as infants, unconditional love and support from our parents, regardless of what we did. Obviously that could never happen perfectly —parents are never perfect—but children are meant to get the message, the internal imprint, in the first few years of their lives, that who they are, as they are, is okay. We all receive this message to a greater or lesser extent. The possibility for a child to mature with a sense of perfect "okay-ness" is arguably nonexistent, while the incidences in which children pass into adolescence with almost no sense of their basic goodness are tragically common. Nevertheless, the most important point to remember is that none of us emerge from childhood completely unscathed, entirely sheltered from a sense of shame, clear of betrayal, or free of the perception that we have failed to meet the expectations of our parents.

The moment at which this wounding occurs becomes a pivot point, a point of significant failure, and it is at this crucial juncture that we make a decision to protect ourselves from future emotional pain. From this point on, the efforts we make to achieve or do anything are oriented toward this wound, toward the perceived lack of love that we experienced as a child. Depending upon the severity of the wound and the tenacity of the protection strategy we put into place, the life that follows that decision, wherever we go and whatever we do, becomes dedicated to finding love "out there," externally, since after the wounding we no longer trust our own "enough-ness," our own wholeness. So we devise ways through our behavior, our attitudes, our postures and personality to try and get that love for ourselves while avoiding the risk of being rejected.

This chronic activity of looking for the love we feel we have lost in childhood creates a split in us. The activity of looking externally for love dissociates us from our own being. We leave ourselves behind when we go searching for it; we abandon who we really are in the hopes of finding it. When we abandon ourselves this way, we lose a spontaneous, direct contact with the simple wisdom of our own body. We mistrust our own thoughts, feelings and behavior, since we are unsure whether or not they will lead us into further pain; we second-guess, cover up and adapt our manifestations to what we believe will satisfy the "adults" with whom we are interacting. The art of staying home is about the reclamation of who we are, simply as natural, embodied human beings.

When we talk about going back to what we naturally are as human beings, though it sounds simple, we are up against an extremely powerful force, a survival strategy to which just the idea of being naturally undefended and vulnerably authentic will provoke a terror that is linked up to this experience of being unloved. As a result, we have this literal dissociation from our naturally vibrant and alive human disposition. How we relate to everyone in our lives—our parents, our mate, our children, our friends—is rooted in this dissociation where our attention, which should be free and open and responsive, is turned neurotically toward the "other," not from the standpoint of being considerate of them, but from the perspective of needing something from them or at least, at a subtle level of paranoia, scheming to avoid their criticism, judgment or rejection.

Not to belabor the point, it's important for us to see the background against which we have projected ourselves outward toward the pursuit of satisfaction, fulfillment or "liberation." We have internalized the worldview that actualization has escaped us and must be retrieved, and we are therefore in search of it.

The work of the one percent is to move from this dissociated and split condition into a natural and ordinary association with our bodies. If we try to develop a direct relationship to the miracle, magic and grace part of this whole path, we will fail, because it is unmappable, uncontainable, and it has no feature to which we can grab on with our human senses.

Fortunately, the one percent, which is called *kaya sadhana*, or cultivation of the body, is a science. It is tremendously precise, exacting, and lawful, which means we can actually practice it. The elements of this practice involve an intentional relationship to formal meditation, diet, study, relationship, exercise, and livelihood. Each of these intentionally lived activities is designed to support a radical realization in the core practice of meditation; they provide the matrix in which transformation can arise and then be integrated and lived.

These practices, if engaged devotedly and properly, however, bring no gain for us as practitioners—at least no gain in the ways we have been trained to perceive profit, accomplishment and value. We just get an ordinary life—a life in which we're not running around all the time, distracting ourselves and blindly effecting the habits we learned as children, habits of a thousand forms of dissociation.

The practices are very simple, very basic, very sane. We'll talk more specifically about them later. In fact, they're so simple and so basic and so sane that it really causes us some wonder when our attempts to simply stick to those practices create such panic. Anyone who has attempted regular meditation can attest to the fact that just the simple act of sitting in one place for an hour of time can produce tremendous discomfort. And if we try seriously to engage the practices of basic human sanity as many wisdom traditions suggest we engage them, whether it is the Ten Commandments or the principles of Buddhism, we will begin to discover that the resistance we have to a simple, basic life is very great. And our resistance is all based on a belief that if we stop our search we will die.

Even though doing these practices and coming into a simple relationship to this body we inhabit seems as though it would be a death to us, its actual result is an intimate relationship to ourselves in our simplicity. For instance, if we stopped eating all sorts of strange, sugary, junky foods, we would, over a period of time, gradually find our whole brain chemistry stabilizing; our thinking process would become less volatile, and we might even be disturbed at first by this quietude, much the way a city person might find it hard to sleep for the first few nights in the country.

How to Be Found

If you've ever been in a busy shopping center with a friend, you may have experienced the frustration of trying to reunite after getting unintentionally separated. Both parties, having lost their partner, are faced with a dilemma: Do I look all over the shopping mall for my friend, or sit in one place and trust that when he/she realizes we've become separated he/she will come looking for me?

Given that the mall has limits, regardless of its size, if one person stays in one place while the other does the looking, the "lost one" will eventually be found, even if the "seeker" has to look everywhere else first.

Now expand this dynamic to the level of the entire universe. We have become separated from the divine—from ourselves in the form of our "true nature" or reality. Even in the shopping mall, if both parties are actively looking for each other, the possibility exists of never finding each other again. But given the entire universe, if we *and* the divine are looking for each other, the chances of our meeting up on some street corner are astoundingly remote. For this reason the spiritual path has a "golden rule" which is meant to streamline this process of our reconnection:

It is the divine that does the looking. Not us.

Kaya sadhana is the science of how to stay in one place in the shopping center after we get separated from our natural state. It's the science of being where we're supposed to be when the divine comes to look for us; that is, rooted in, anchored in and tethered to ordinary human embodiment, not distracted, dissociated, entertained, pleasured or numbed away from that embodiment.

Our culture is unaware of this principle, however. We're out there searching in a million ways, "looking for love in all the wrong faces, looking for love in too many places," as the song goes; not at home; weeping and wailing and gnashing our teeth, when all the while the divine has been to our house fifty times in the last three weeks, but we weren't there. We were out looking for it.

Here in This Body

This is literally what we are doing. The very dynamic of our attention being elsewhere, and not just here in this body, makes it impossible for the divine to find us. A book that Osho Rajneesh put out a long time ago features the title, *Don't Just Do Something, Sit There.* That title describes precisely what the discipline of meditation is about: developing the art of staying home.

Out of habit we spread ourselves thin, stretching horizontally, trying to cover all the bases, reach all the destinations available to us—amassing frequent flyer points for ever more exploration. But that exploration is one-dimensional until we allow ourselves to drop within and to discover a deep well of life that we have been sitting on all along. To stay home is to explore ourselves as depth, not just as the lure to ever-new horizons.

Meditation is the practice of giving all our weight to the spot we currently occupy, to inhabit it with the full measure of our gravity. Our beliefs and ideas about ourselves are an artificial floor which cannot hold up beneath the full weight of our presence. If we allow that presence, that floor inevitably gives way and we fall through to the solid ground of a simple and direct relationship to ourselves, unmediated by the middleman of self-image and the protection of that image.

There is one possible outcome of breaking through to the territories of reality, and that is suffering. Most of our so-called search for love is based on a life that we are running from: the life that happened to us when we were children. We hope that we can find a different life without having to go back to the pain of the past, but the key to our future growth has been left behind, buried at the bottom of that heap of fear, anguish and sorrow. When we agree to stay home and to accept an intimate relationship to ourselves, we take responsibility for all the experiences and the circumstances that we've been trying to avoid. We agree to a relationship to all that we wanted to wall out, and the result of that relating is *feeling*—feeling which will come to us, in part, as suffering.

Meditation is the posture in which we can bear this suffering and transmute it into an expansive context. Suffering borne in a posture of denial or contraction is like a scream in an echo chamber; there is nothing to help us absorb its magnitude. Suffering held in the context of meditation is like a cry in the woods—that pain is heard by the nature of life itself; there is an abundance of natural law present to bear witness to the cry, and that witness is tremendously nurturing. Instead of echoing back at us, the pain is received and grounded.

In *Zen Mind, Beginner's Mind,* Suzuki Roshi, one of the forefathers of American Zen, says, "In the zazen posture, your mind and body have great power to accept things as they are, whether agreeable or disagreeable." [1]

Just like that, there is ninety-nine percent of the path that we longer have to worry about. We don't have to understand anything other than how to practice the one percent. When we become responsible for the practice of staying home in the body, the glory of spiritual life unfolds naturally, guided by the creative intelligence of the divine itself, which happily carries us and moves us once it discovers that we are doing our part—that we have learned how to be present and to relax into the arms of real help.

CHAPTER THREE

There Is No Good Reason to Meditate

We all start out as a "closet case." We have a secret life with secret pain that we keep under wraps in this closet. We bolt the door and hide the key, keeping our dark side hidden away, and we work very hard to function over the top of that pain, fear and anguish and go on somehow with our lives, perhaps thinking we are the only ones with secret pain.

In conventional therapy—much of which is disguised as spirituality in the West—we get empowered, encouraged, supported, loved and affirmed in such a way that we are able to clean out that closet. The old baggage—the past, our low self-esteem, our trauma—all get lovingly removed, cleaned, pressed, folded, our wardrobe is updated, and the result is a closet into which the greater society and our loved ones can safely look.

In the process of true transformation, however, the authentic path tells us to leave everything in the closet alone and to not do *anything* with it. In addition, it casually suggests that we might want to just go sit in the closet for a while until we find a new relationship to all of the stuff in it.

Now neither we, nor society, nor our loved ones want a *relationship* to the stuff in our closet, in its current condition. We want to get the hell out of the closet, leave it behind, bulldoze it under and be done with it, so that's tricky. But if we're lucky, and maybe a bit of a black sheep anyhow, we may actually try "just sitting" in it. And perhaps we find out that it's not as bad as we imagined and we sit in there some more. Then perhaps our eyes adjust in the darkness and we start to notice things in there we hadn't seen before. And we sit in there and sit in there and just when it seems as though it is in fact a pointless activity, one day a bolt of lightning blazes out of our boxer shorts (or some other place we least expected) and that bolt vaporizes the closet *itself* as the container of all this mess, shatters it into nothingness, *without touching any of the stuff that's been inside it.*

At that point we are wholly (and holy) "out of the closet," and even though those who come to visit us are going to judge us by the fact that the *contents* of our closet remain intact and unchanged, we are going to experience our own life in a very different way. We are going to see that all this stuff doesn't belong to *anyone,* and that we were identified with the closet itself, thinking that all this stuff was in *us.* Suddenly, instead of darkness, there is going to be air, warm sunlight and acceptance—acceptance even of the non-acceptance that used to be inside our closet and still exists, but not inside *anything,* not belonging to *anyone* or having *any essential location.*

The highest function of meditation is to eradicate every plank of the closet of identity such that we are no longer shielded from the open sky of reality. Then all of the stuff we'd been obsessing over and trying to change just *is*, but it's not in *us*. In fact there is no "I" that could contain it or associate itself with that content. When we're not buffered by our closet of conditioning and mistaken identity, we simply put up an umbrella if it's raining. When it's sunny we put on a bathing suit. Life is suddenly very straightforward.

Transformation is not what happens once we've "changed"; it's coming out of the dark and seeing what we've got and relating to it appropriately and clearly. If we've got a funnel in our hands but we think it's a bucket, we're going to keep losing things we value. If we know we've got a funnel, then we stick one finger in the hole and use it like a bucket to get by in the absence of one. We're "transformed" when we fully know who we are—or, even more important, who we are not.

The result of deep meditation is not a "result" at all, but the revealing of a condition that existed prior to our adoption of the idea that something special was needed to fix us, repair us, or restore us to happiness. The belief in our brokenness is the position from which we start making all kinds of demands on ourselves and then eventually projecting those demands onto others and all of life. This prior condition is extraordinarily simple and free not only from the demand for wealth, stress-free living, health, popularity, excitement and true love, but essentially free from *all* demands and expectations. At the same time, this condition leaves us utterly free to entertain preferences, intentions and aims. This thing called transformation is simply not what we've come to think it is.

When Suzuki Roshi was once asked about enlightenment, he purportedly remarked, "What do you want to know for? You may not like it."[1] My own teacher, Lee Lozowick, has commented, "Realization is not very exciting. Everybody is already Realized anyway. What's the big deal? You're just exactly as you are. That's not exciting; it's simply natural."[2]

So, yes, the path is the goal, there is nothing other than this, and looking for and expecting some kind of reward in the future is the surest way to have it elude us. Our search for "enlightenment" is about as justifiable as it would be for Newt Gingrich to be searching for unique surnames; what we're looking for is already true of us. Yet . . . it generally takes *time*, plain old effort, and persistence to find that out, to *fully open* to the fact that the future payoff is not there, will never be there, and then to surrender to that as a whole-body realization. Effortless effort, as the Zen maxim goes, is required.

Meditation is the invitation we give the universe to use us, to make us a tool of revolutionary benefit to the world as it exists. To quote Lee Lozowick again, "You just need to leave a crack for God." Meditation can be the crack, the doorway, and eventually the canyon we open in our heart and our attention for the divine so that we can be joined to the process which is all around us that we call life. May this book serve your path and the one path we all share—willing or not!

What Is Mind?

❧

CHAPTER FOUR

You Had
to Be There

If we want to know what the mind is, it stands to reason that we have to find what it is that the mind arises *within,* exactly the way we would examine the whole of a sentence to come to a right understanding of the use of a word within it. We call this "context."

We could investigate what the mind essentially is from many different perspectives. We could research the physiology which gives rise to various neural impulses, chemical reactions and electrical activity in various parts of the brain. We could look up scientific studies that could describe for us in great detail which lobes and hemispheres become active during what kinds of activities, what the differences are between men and women, and even find out exactly what part of the brain needs to be stimulated in order to have certain thoughts or feelings.

We could investigate the "truth" of the mind from a cultural perspective, investigating how our social environment and upbringing have shaped our likes, dislikes, thinking patterns, mental development, sense of self and so on.

Regardless, however, to what extent we study, research and educate ourselves about how the mind works, until we begin to observe ourselves from an interior vantage point we will be short of crucial knowledge with respect to the workings of our mind. Science can give us a tremendous amount of information which in itself is very useful, but all of that information can only describe the externally visible manifestations of mind. As far as data goes, science has gone beyond the call of duty in providing its share of the facts.

So through study and research we can come to know the physics which the mind arises in, we can know the culture which it arises in, we can know the biology which it arises in, we can know the geography, climate and environment which it arises in, but without an interior view of the mind itself, we cannot come to know the *consciousness* which it arises in— simply because, to date, science has not been able to develop instrumentation which can duplicate the conscious mind itself as a research tool. Just as a scientist, with training, can accurately study and then report upon his or her findings, giving an accurate contextual report in their field of expertise, so can an experienced and properly trained meditator gain direct access to the context of consciousness. And just as only other trained scientists are able to verify or refute the findings of experts in their own field, so only can an accomplished meditator verify the discoveries of another meditator.

As Ken Wilber suggests in *A Brief History of Everything,*

If you want to know what these men and women are actually talking about, then you must take up the con-

templative practice or injunction or paradigm, and perform the experiment yourself. These archetypes, the
true archetypes, are a meditative experience, and it is
very hard to understand these archetypes without performing the experiment. They are not images existing
in the mythic worldspace, they are not philosophical
concepts existing in the rational worldspace; they are
meditative phenomena existing in the subtle worldspace. [1]

This is where we run into difficulty. The study of the con-
texts in which observable matter arises is empirical; that is,
those studies produce evidence that is also observable to
others: pictures, electrical activity, statistical data, flowcharts
—all confirm the findings of the researcher. The meditator,
however, can walk away from twenty years of intensive research with absolutely nothing to show for it other than a
beatific grin, which qualifies in few laboratories as empirical
evidence.

Mostly what we have as a result of consciousness research,
or meditation, are religious texts, scripture, poetry or *dharma*
[spiritual teachings]. But this material is not verifiable in any
laboratory except the one in which we live. In short, the context in which consciousness arises can only be *experienced*
by one scientist at a time. In addition, that scientist has to be
tiny enough to get inside our body and patient enough to sit
around doing nothing for what may take hundreds or thousands of hours, without reading a magazine, without taking
breaks. And the scientist has to remain alert, because the
doorway behind which the context of consciousness is waiting to reveal itself could open at any minute. The Sufi tradition says that door opens once in a hundred years. Where

are we going to find such a scientist to conduct this kind of research project? We could write up a proposal to try to get funding for one, but chances are there are few organizations likely to be interested in underwriting the project. This is why, if we are truly interested in the experiment, that scientist always winds up in the end being ourselves. We cannot know the context of consciousness except by direct observation and experience.

The research which can be shared by those who do meditate is a very different category of data. It is not delivered linearly by empirical means, but is demonstrated, lived and transmitted through relationship, mood, impressions, feelings, hints and metaphors. If our evidence of a microbiological discovery rested on a laboratory slide, we could let anyone borrow our high-powered microscope to view it. Not so of course at the level of consciousness. The equipment needed to view the subtlety of consciousness is not transferable, not to be given; it must be *developed*, which is why most people who attempt to share their own experience of meditation in words usually wind up tripping over their tongue in frustration and, quite appropriately, finally declaring, "You had to be there."

We can, however, talk about the observable features of the mind we all share in such a way that entices us to investigate on our own behalf so that we may come to know for ourselves what the mind is. We can remind ourselves that the mind is trainable, that we have possibilities we may have forgotten about, experiences we may have been ignoring that are important openings. We can rock the boat of our conventional thinking, and sometimes we can even capsize that boat and have a refreshing dip in a new way of looking at things. We don't even have to make any hard and fast claims

—we can simply talk about how the mind seems to be in our own experience, from an interior perspective, and just this can be of tremendous value.

Finally, however, we're going to have to walk into the cage of mind and face it ourselves if we really want to know what the mind is, not through the veil of concepts and theories but directly and unquestionably, which is what meditation is all about. We might once again listen to Ken Wilber.

So, if you're skeptical, that's a healthy attitude, and we invite you to find out for yourself, and perform this interior experiment with us, and get the data, and help us interpret it. But if you won't perform the experiment, please don't ridicule those who do.[2]

CHAPTER FIVE

What Do We Have In Mind?

Generative Mind and Receptive Mind

We might say there are two types of mind within us—the mind that is generative and the mind that is receptive. Generative mind is like an ice cream truck with no brakes: full of great ideas, thoughts and plans, yet none of it can be accessed, because this type of mind never slows down enough for us to be able to get at the goodies. Because it is constantly generating product that can't be unloaded, the truck fills up, the driver is forced off the vehicle altogether, and in the end we have an overflowing factory of theory that is completely out of control and that eventually causes all kind of damage when it crashes into our actual lives.

Generative mind is the type of mind that keeps us awake at night, playing nonexistent chess games with the circumstances of our lives. Generative mind becomes particularly active when we've activated a flight or fight response through some concern that we've identified as being linked to our survival. The problem is that generative mind doesn't make distinctions between the survival of the body—of who we are as functional individuals—and survival of ego, our current self-image, our beliefs and cultural conditioning. Generative mind will apply the same vehemence to figuring out how to avoid a conversation with a person who threatens us as it would how to escape a concentration camp; the same level of emergency to obtaining the right breakfast food as to avoiding a car crash.

Generative mind makes us restless, jumpy, edgy; it inappropriately charges the nervous system with unnecessary tension, and it is primarily the alleviation of these effects for which meditation has become most known and practiced in the West. While the quelling of this agitation is certainly a fringe benefit of a meditation practice, to stop when we begin to experience a relative degree of peace and calm would be like agreeing to have sex with our mate and then going to sleep as soon as we've reached the bed because it's so warm and cozy. We've forgotten our true purpose! It's the same for meditation. Peace and calm is often a side effect, but much more is possible on the cushion than just that. Overcoming generative mind is only an initial step in the process of transformation. When the mind stops racing all over the place, we're just at a starting point with respect to what is possible in meditation.

Receptive mind is more like a Salvation Army van. This vehicle always departs empty—*begins with emptiness*—and drives around the neighborhood picking up all those things which would otherwise be discarded. The mission of this vehicle is to see the value of these things, recognize the beauty of them; it dusts things off, turns them over, appreciates their possibility and can apply the already established presence of existing realities to the needs of the moment or distribute them to benefit others. Receptive mind doesn't miss what is already there—whereas generative mind is interested only in the newest, shiniest version of whatever is available.

The Mind As Salesman

The mind that is generative is also the low-wage front counter help in the establishment where life is served up to the masses. It seems that this counter clerk is on commission and has completed a number of certification courses in the art of "horizontal marketing": the offer of options, accessories, augmentations, upgrades and alternatives to the original, basic product of reality. Any attempt to order life just as it is, nothing added, nothing subtracted, sounds something like this:

"Hello. I'd like one order of reality," you say.

The clerk turns toward you with a big smile and then, with a smooth "just-aimin'-to-please" tone, responds. "Certainly! And what would you like with that?"

"Oh!" you exclaim, a bit taken aback. "I didn't know there were options."

Then, flashing a row of perfect teeth, which puts you a little more at ease, he croons, "No options? Why, of course, there are options—and plenty of them I might add. The special today is your basic order of reality smothered with a thick layer of sweet, melted sentimentality."

"Oh, gosh," you exclaim. "Well, sounds interesting, but . . . I think I'll just take the basic reality."

"Certainly. Oh, by the way, we also have a standing special, as long as quantities last, on spicy criticism. Gives a very nice little kick to our basic product. In fact, those who have tried it just a couple of times say they'd never go back to having reality just plain without it."

"Well, thanks, but no thanks."

Now you have your money out with just the right amount of change for the order of basic reality, which you've placed on the counter to indicate your certainty and to combat the apparent pushiness of this clerk. "Just this, please," you say assertively.

"As you wish," the clerk replies, still smooth as can be without missing a beat. He reaches behind him and quick as a flash drops something on the counter that hits the surface with a rock-like crack and then tumbles to a stop.

You pick it up to examine it and find it to be at sub-zero temperature. "This is freezing," you tell him.

"Yes. That's the basic. An order of cold hard reality."

"But I didn't order cold hard reality," you shoot back. "I just wanted regular reality."

"I'm sorry, sir, that's how we ship it and store it. If you'd like it any other way, you'll have to pay extra."

"Can I just have it warmed up a bit? Give it a slight thaw?" you beg.

Then the clerk leans over the counter and whispers to you, "Just between you and me, I wouldn't take it plain if I were you. It's honestly rather bland if you ask me. I shouldn't be telling you this, but you might want to take a little something additional with it."

You finally relent. "All right, then, just for curiosity's sake, what are the options?"

At this your salesperson absolutely lights up, swelling to an unusual height and spreading his arms wide. Throwing the switch to a neon sign board above the counter, he starts singing the McDonald's theme song. *"You deserve a break today, so get up and get away to . . . some options!"* Then he jumps up on the counter. Three hundred balloons plus confetti descend from the ceiling. Scantily clad dancing girls hover on each of his arms. He twirls them and pirouettes over to a waiting microphone, where he booms over the loudspeakers:

We're proud in our establishment to help you
  to re-orient
from the simple truth of the things you see to
  a more complex reality—
from the boring fact of simple things to the adrenal
  rush that desire brings.
We can take your day as it's been given and help
  you feel a bit more driven.

 Why settle for life, as it is? We'll give you hopes
  you can't outlive.
 Why be with yourself just as you are, when in
  your mind you can be a star?
 We've products you can smear and spread, cuddle
  close and take to bed.
 You'll be the envy of all in town, in your color
  of choice, no money down.

 Criticisms, doubts and fears, we'll match for
  you illusions
 which perfectly suit your temperament and your
  self-delusions.
 No need to balk, now don't delay to buy into
  our schemes.
 We're Mind Inc. and our motto is: "We turn
  your truth to dreams."

So what is the mind trying to sell us? And if it's true that the mind is trying to sell us something that we may or may not need, what would it mean to become educated buyers?

The Mind As Interpreter

Werner Erhard called the mind a "meaning making machine." If we want to become educated buyers with respect to what the mind generates for our potential investment, we need to understand its obsessive compulsion with the creation of meaning. If we don't understand this at the outset, we make the mistake of assuming that the meaning aspect of what the mind puts forth is inherent rather than generated by the mind itself. These generated meanings are the very building blocks of illusion.

If we've attempted meditation at all, or any degree of self-observation, we come to know that we are fraught with concern. The word "fraught" is actually an acronym standing for the Free and Random Association of Unconsciously Generated and Habitual Thought. We can see why this phrase became abbreviated as an acronym; nevertheless, we are faced with the fact that the mind is a very hard worker and that, in fact, it seldom takes a break. As Sir George Jessel observed, "The human brain starts working the moment you are born, and never stops until you stand up to speak in public."

So unless we are speaking in public, we have a "free-thinker" on our hands whom we need to grapple with if we ever hope to create some breathing space for ourselves within.

This process of free-thinking or free association occurs in our absence. We are not "paying" attention, the thinking and association is therefore "free" in that moment, but the cost is incurred later. It is after we have fallen prey to some meaning which has been assumed or associated into place that we lose the key to the door of presence. So one of the first things we need to observe and discover about ourselves on this path is the undisciplined nature of our own mind that produces these assumptions.

Try answering each of the following questions aloud to yourself. What is the largest appliance in a kitchen? What is the most common color this appliance comes in? What do cows drink? Cows, of course, drink water. But if you answered "milk," you've just proven for yourself how difficult it is for our mind to operate outside of its mechanical process of making associations.

This, after all, is one of the mind's jobs: to provide an endless stream of associations which are designed to afford us the opportunity to draw upon our vast experience to help us navigate successfully and safely through life. This, of course, is a good thing. When we become absent, however, and this process occurs automatically without a master, then associations turn into *assumptions,* and we are suddenly mistaking a whole range of proposed interpretations which may arise in any given moment for reality itself. This is where the trouble begins. The untrained mind generates one assumption after another, based on the random firing of associations that just get put together any which way they get joined up, without examination.

Of course, our tendency is to favor those associations that support the worldviews we believe in; happily jumping to conclusions that give us the go-ahead for our point of view. As one comedian commented on the subject of vegetarianism, "If God didn't want us to eat animals, he wouldn't have made them out of meat." The absurdity of our own co-opted use of logic is the basis of some very good comedy. Yet, make a few minor substitutions—for instance, "If God wanted me to be kind to my boss, he wouldn't have made him such an asshole," or "If God wanted me to be in this relationship he wouldn't have made it so painful"—and suddenly we're not laughing anymore. When we are identified with our conclusions and perceptions, the cause of our suffering is no longer transparent and obvious.

The unconscious mind is no more than the collection of these arbitrary conditioned responses that leap into the foreground in reaction to "what is." The mechanical barrage of associations that apply themselves with tremendous intensity to the moment, even before we get a chance to truly experience it, buries us underneath a mound of preconditioning. Then we relate to "what is" based on whatever is at the top of the pile.

An untrained or unmastered mind is constantly being led away into identification with that which is essentially an illusion. The mind that cannot see through to the impermanence of things does not see things the way they *are* (changing and passing), and therefore cannot achieve what the East Indian sage Swami Papa Ramdas calls the "fullness of experience" which leads to liberation.

> Even the repeated experience of the transient nature of the objects to which a man is attached, does not strike off the veil of Maya that clouds his vision. For, ignorance is not an easy thing to conquer and dispel; it eclipses the bright vision he has had from time to time, dragging him down again and again. Hence *fullness* of experience alone rends and destroys once for all the veil of ignorance.[1]

It is only a fullness of experience that has the power and presence to overcome the domination of interpretation that normally exerts itself over and against our clarity. This fullness of presence comes into maturity relative to the degree that we are able to make a conscious and passionate admission that our interpretations of reality could be wrong, and become willing to look past all the "certainties" we have collected in our hip pocket to ward off the discomfort of dealing with the unknown itself.

The practice of meditation is a prescription for the runaway disease of assumption-making, a kind of spiritual battering ram that is ever available to knock down the assumptions we habitually erect in response to our experiences and life circumstances. Such assumptions block our ability to rest in the divine itself, to ride the comet tail of the unknown as it speeds ahead. The evolution of creative intelligence is not to be understood or captured by any story we make up about the significance or meaning of the moment, so all of our assumptions must be pierced and left behind from instant to instant if we wish to support the unfolding of that evolution.

The basis upon which we rest in presence requires a fundamental understanding of the law of impermanence. As long as we believe that the conclusions we're drawing are permanent or "real," we're tempted to do something with them, build something upon them, invest in them. If the interpretation is pleasurable, we want to protect the experience or even try to make it permanent. This leads to craving. If the interpretation is negative, we want to change or alter our life circumstance to suit our preferences or make it go away altogether. This leads to aversion. Craving and aversion are reactive tendencies that sow the seed for all other forms of faulty discrimination and the taking of inappropriate action. It is our belief in the substantiality of passing phenomena and our conditioned responses to those phenomena that make the grail of reality seem elusive and mythical.

The drama of our separate lives is like a projected movie. If we are disturbed by it, put off balance, lost to our true selves in it, then we will inevitably take inappropriate action, trying to defend ourselves against that which is only an illusion. We may keep trying to break into the projection room to sabotage the machine, obsessively plot over ways we could assassinate the projectionist, file a lawsuit against the theater, or enter into endless debate over whose fault it is that we are so miserable. In actuality, however, all we have to do is take down the screen of identification by becoming present, so that regardless of what gets projected there is nothing off which the drama can reflect.

The fact that our mind is continuously generating random assumptions that do not in any way reflect reality is a primary obstacle or dynamic that, through practice, we must be able to reliably transcend in order to become available to ourselves, to our partners, to our children and friends, to creative intelligence, and to life itself.

CHAPTER SIX

The Chain of Reaction

Let's take an even closer look at the mechanics of the mind. Gautama Buddha, through the process of meditation and self-observation, mapped out four distinct parts of the mind. What we have come to experience as one lightning-fast process of thinking has, in fact, distinct elements. The only way to observe these elements as being discrete and to attain the capacity to bring our awareness into the midst of the mind's dynamic is to observe the process ourselves. But it can be useful to begin our observation with a skeleton sense of the mind's structure. The four parts of the mind delineated by Buddha are *consciousness, perception, sensation,* and *reaction.*

Let's take an ordinary daily example and examine how these four functions of mind work. Let us say we're driving down a two-lane boulevard, enjoying the sight of newly blossoming cherry trees planted all along the median for half a mile.

Consciousness sees the cherry trees, the fluffy shapes of the pink blooms, the thick blanket of fallen petals that have carpeted the ground like magenta snow; that's all. The job of consciousness is simple: to receive the raw data.

Perception recognizes the trees as something it has seen before, remembers being close to the blossoms of a cherry tree on one occasion, and recalls how heavenly its flowers smelled; it also then remembers a first kiss beneath a cherry tree. *Oh, that was nice, that was a pleasant experience.* Perception has now completed its job by assigning the cognition an overall value. These cherry trees are *good,* and not only are they just good, they are good the way a kiss is good. An association has been made to an extremely favorable activity.

Suddenly, *sensation* steps in, shoving perception out of the way. "I'll take it from here," it commands. The assigning of value is sensation's go-ahead to flood the body with feelings —in this case, pleasant ones. Even though we are only driving past the cherry trees, the body is practically swooning in delight at the perfume of the flowers, which is only being remembered, and our heart is racing with excitement as if that first kiss were still sweet on our lips.

Remember, this is all happening very quickly. Consciousness, perception and sensation may get less than a fraction of a second in the driver's seat before the last part of the mind, *reaction,* has kicked them all entirely aside and assumes charge of the entire episode.

Reaction now wants to make this feeling *last.* It craves more of this good feeling. It *wants* the cherry tree, and wants it like it wants the sweetness and excitement of that first kiss. Reaction is the jealous lover that will stop at nothing to secure its source of pleasure or distance itself from pain. Whatever the line of association, it is fueled by the mind's unconscious addiction to having pleasant feelings and sensations.

Suddenly a car comes zooming by us on the right. It passes us going about twenty miles an hour faster and, once by, the car swerves into our lane and stops, presumably about to make a left-hand turn onto a side street but waiting for oncoming traffic to clear. We apply the brakes sharply and squeal to a halt behind the car, inches away from the bumper.

Consciousness sees that the car is traveling faster than we are and that the car is blue. *Perception* says, "That car is going *too* fast, that's dangerous, that's *bad.*" *Sensation* starts creating knots in our stomach, tightness in the chest. *Reaction* then sets in: "This must be stopped. People cannot be allowed to drive this way." We note the license number and reach for our cell phone to notify 911, but before we can do that the car has swerved in front of us and we curse the driver loudly as we jump on the brake.

We saw the car swerve in front of us; that's *consciousness.* We labeled the actions of the driver not only hazardous, but because we had already experienced negative feelings about the driver, his behavior now gets a worse than bad ranking by *perception;* it is inexcusable. *Sensation* then immediately pushes the emergency adrenaline button because perception stamped "very bad" on the event. *Reaction* then shouts at the driver before we even have time to think about what we're doing.

As the car finally turns, it becomes obvious that there are two policemen in uniform in the front seat of an unmarked patrol car apparently responding to an emergency. Now we feel not only angry, but foolish as well.

And this is just a snapshot of our day. By the end of it, consciousness has yielded the floor to an untold number of perceptions, most of them incorrect, an unruly herd of sensations and reactions has stampeded through the body, and we wonder at our exhaustion.

If we want to remain present in the moment, consciousness must develop some authority. We need to able, at any given point in the process of "thinking," to insert consciousness back into the equation. Otherwise, we perceive and react to nonexistent problems and engage in all kinds of self-created suffering when we already have plenty of *real* suffering to work with, thank you very much. As Mark Twain observed, "I am an old man and have known a great many troubles, but most of them have never happened."

To reassert consciousness, if we begin judging something as being good or bad, we simply recognize that we're having a judgment about that person or situation. If we are experiencing sensations as a result of a value judgment, we become conscious of the actual physical sensations we are experiencing and we rest in those sensations as they are, *fully feeling them.* If we begin to react to those sensations by wanting more or less of them, we simply observe, "I'm reacting, isn't that interesting?"

Part of the difficulty is that the part of the mind that issues sensations is very sloppy. We can have a fleeting thought, barely worth our attention, and this part of the mind sends a marching band to deliver the message that something is happening when a telegram would have sufficed.

I live very near the border between Canada and the United States. Crossing into either country I always experience sensations of anxiety when I pass through customs, especially if the line is long. There I am, inching along, with plenty of time to look ahead and watch the customs agents grill every driver with stern expressions. I know the tone of their questioning is going to be intimidating; it's meant to be, I suppose. "You've nothing to hide," I remind myself, yet why then do I get so nervous? By the time I get to the front of the line, I *want* to be guilty of something.

Even though sensations are assigned inaccurately, their nature is so convincing that we often redefine ourselves or our worldview to legitimize them. This is the entire basis of marketing, which works by first creating a strong experience of sensation for its audience and then providing an interpretation of that sensation which favors acting on behalf of the product.

A man who claimed to dislike animals was challenged to a bet by a friend. The bet was that the friend, by placing a single item in the man's home, could force him to get a pet. The man instantly accepted, vowing that he would never give in. Once the stakes were agreed upon, the friend arrived at the man's home with a beautiful silver birdcage, which he hung in a corner of the living room.

"I can see what you're doing," the man said, "but it will never work. I will never get a bird."

But after several weeks of looking at the cage every day, the man for the first time noticed a pet store in his neighborhood. After a while he started looking at the parrots in the window as he passed. When friends came over to his house, they would always ask, "What happened to your bird? Did he die?" and then the man would have to explain the whole story. Gradually, the cage became such a focus of his attention and the lack of having a bird was such an inconvenience that the man finally relented and bought one of the parrots.

The sensations in our body are like an empty birdcage. They show up in the living room of our attention and we unconsciously oblige them by "purchasing the bird." If they're sensations of anxiety, for example, we find something worth worrying about. If they're sensations of craving, we locate something or someone to lust over.

At any stage of the mind's process we can re-anchor the authority of consciousness by recognizing what is true in that instant, what the body is experiencing and what the mind is doing, and being with it *without judgment.* The moment we begin judging, we open the gates for the horse race of perception, sensation and reaction. There is a lot of heat and passion and excitement in that race, and before you know it we're invested in some outcome, we've got our money on a winner, and whether we win or lose, we're riding the roller coaster of craving and aversion.

Any time we observe any facet of this process without judgment, we are feeding the authority of consciousness. The trick is to know that we can stop judging at any stage. Even if we are having a judgment about our judgment, it only requires one application of *no judgment* to right the whole boat of consciousness. A sense of humor is a precious commodity in such circumstances. If we can find humor in the situation, we can often interrupt the feeding frenzy of judgment and scatter the vultures of reaction by seeing the absurdity and irony of . . . well, wanting to have sex with a cherry tree, for example.

The Alchemy
of Practice

CHAPTER SEVEN

A Delicate Balance

The technique of meditation is the intentional placement of our minds and our bodies in relationship to life. Attitude is to the context of meditation as posture is to the form of meditation. If our body is properly aligned, then formal meditation practice becomes much easier and our efforts find fertile soil. If our attitude and lifestyle are properly aligned, then informal meditation practice in daily life has solid ground on which to stand and can take us more deeply into right living. In the deepest heart of right living is the state of *sahaj samadhi,* or open-eyed, ecstatic awareness.

The alchemy of practice is the intentional alignment of the mind and body to the fact of reality; the practiced orientation to the presently arising truth of the moment at all levels. We can consider meditation practice to be the core of this alchemy, yet there are also supporting practices that are necessary to protect and catalyze the subtle chemistry that can be the basis of transformation or breakthrough to the realization of nonduality, the ever-present kiss of divine communion.

Each of us as individuals has the responsibility of managing the delicate balance between the application of *discipline*— the ability to hold ourselves to the commitments and boundaries which delineate a strong practice—and *relaxation,* the internal and external atmosphere of expansiveness and inclusiveness out of which surrender into a radically new context could arise.

As we discussed earlier, our habit is to attempt to handle aspects of our development which are out of our hands while giving too much latitude to many of our own behaviors which are begging for self-mastery. In other words, most of us could completely transform our life of practice by seeing that we are far too hard on ourselves in areas where we should lighten up, and far too easy on ourselves in areas where we should fortify our discipline.

Examples of ways in which we are unnecessarily harsh with ourselves tend to be mostly psychological; we give too much rope to our conditioned patterns of neurosis. The way we think about ourselves and the degree to which we allow self-judgment, self-criticism (which often takes the form of criticism of others), and even self-hatred to corner and lecture us is one example of an area which deserves the spaciousness of our nurturing attention. These internal voices can be relaxed, and even dismissed from showing up for work altogether, with nothing but positive results for our life of practice. Eventually, we can replace those "drivers" with their healthy counterparts: self-judgment becomes discrimination; self-criticism becomes compassion and forgiveness; and self-hatred becomes the powerful intention for change.

The frequenting of environments or company that feeds any level of self-limiting or self-defeating tendencies we may already have is another way we can be too hard on ourselves. Such an environment can straightjacket our intention for growth with an unconscious agreement to hold low expectations for each other. The opposite may also be true if we are enmeshed in a dynamic internally or with others where our expectations are too high. If the result of our having high expectations is consistent failure accompanied by any degree of depression, frustration and the obfuscation of well-being, then we are being too hard on ourselves.

We are most often too easy on ourselves in areas of external discipline. Commitments to our meditation practice in the areas of frequency, duration and posture are especially important to honor and protect if we want a strong practice. If we tell ourselves we are going to sit for fifty minutes, become agitated after sitting for fifteen, and then give ourselves the leeway to stop, we send a strong message to the unconscious that our commitments can be "bought" or eroded by certain emotions, moods, concerns or physical sensations.

When we commit to sitting for a certain length of time at a certain time of day—and commit to some frequency in doing this—it is of utmost importance that we follow through with our plans. Advanced stages of practice require us to do battle with extremely powerful internal "entities," forces within us that represent not our conscious life, but our unconscious motives. It is at the foundational levels of practice that we build a track record—credibility with our unconscious—so that when it comes time for us to take a stand with those powerful negative influences, we have some clout, some muscle of will that has been developed in our early stages of practice. When we tell ourselves, "I'm only stopping a few minutes early," or "I've only missed a few days of practice," we leave the forces of the unconscious largely in control and happily comfortable with things. We then make the mistake of thinking that *we* are comfortable and happy with our practice.

Often, when we begin making even these small commitments to practice and following through with them regardless of our prevailing mood or preference, we can seem to feel very uncomfortable, irritable or uneasy. It is, in fact, the forces of sloth, pride and indulgence which become cranky and intolerant when we show follow-through with our practice, and over time we learn to tell the difference between the acrimonious voices of those entities and the call of our heart, which wants transformation and evolution.

In the meantime, these unconscious forces are constantly playing games with us. They sit around having coffee, and if we show even a little bit of determination to rein them in, they lift a pinky finger in response and laugh when we go running away.

We could be sitting in meditation, having done so several days in a row at the same time for a predetermined length of time, and one of these gremlins might say to the others, "Well, I think that's enough forward momentum for him. It's about time we showed him who's boss, don't you think, boys?" Suddenly we're wondering whether we locked the garage door when we came home last night, and that thought leads to fears over the safety of valuable items we have stored in the garage, which leads us to remember that our car is far past due for an oil change, which reminds us that getting an appointment in our repair shop is easiest to do first thing in the morning. The next thing we know we've jumped up from the meditation cushion, grabbed the phone, and are scheduling a tune-up.

A friend in my practicing group relates a story of how when she first began meditating she would sit with the intention of remaining still, but often found herself cleaning the kitchen or busy around the house before she realized that she had intended to be sitting silently doing nothing. The unconscious dynamic of arising thoughts, making associations, and then moving into action in response to them is revealed to us in situations like this.

The more we dedicate ourselves to our practice, the more the forces of the unconscious rally themselves in opposition to our efforts. If we make the mistake of thinking that when meditation is easy for us we are doing well, we will also tend to miss the fact that when we are having difficulty with our practice, and it requires what Gurdjieff called "super-efforts" to follow through, it may actually be because we are getting results. What we will eventually come to realize is that our freedom is buried beneath layers and layers of justification for not practicing. If we commit to our practice, those justifications are going to surface one by one over a lengthy period of time, disguised in attire we may find difficult to dismiss.

For instance, we may have as much difficulty letting go of our grandmother's way of *thinking* about life as we would giving up an actual family heirloom. Since we inherit family attitudes the same way we acquire family property or physical characteristics, we are prone to their influences, even if those attitudes are inappropriate to our own present-day adult lives. Perhaps our grandmother was the rock who rescued all her children from an abusive father and went around covering their bruised souls with blankets of her nurturing, but also with her denial—not only of the abuse, but of her own pain, her profound sadness.

Sitting practice can trigger a purification not only of our

own psyche and our personal history, but of the past and collective psyche of a whole ancestry, a whole genealogical lineage of tendencies and wounds. Our grandmother's sadness may surface in us as a despair more bottomless than any we have ever known. Still, we do not have to know what it is that is being purified through us or from where it comes. We only have to allow this natural purification to move through us without altering or abandoning our commitment to the nuts and bolts of our practice.

Our purpose, after all, is to root out through the practice of sitting those areas of unconsciousness which keep us stuck in our daily lives. If those forces are being corralled into the atmosphere of formal sitting, we can be grateful that our discipline is provoking them into the arena of practice, where we have a chance to work with them. When the unconscious begins to become conscious it is seldom a pleasant occasion.

Recently, another friend of mine had this experience. After committing to a stronger level of practice and attending a formal meditation period every day for a week, his neck and back went completely out, apparently leaving him no choice but to remain in bed for days on end. While we do have actual physiological symptoms that we should not ignore, sometimes we have to give boundaries to them—agree to pay attention to them and to develop intimacy with them in the context of our practice life—that is, on *our* turf, not on theirs. When we bring these errant parts of ourselves into our meditation practice, we can develop a dialogue with them. We are not turning them out, shunning them, or banishing them when we do this—we are in fact agreeing to a relationship with these parts by inviting them into our sitting practice. There we can acknowledge these parts, witness them as they are, and a healing can take place. If we capitulate to their infantile demands to manipulate and dominate our lives, however, we are not healing them at all, but are only allowing those entities to spin infinitely tangled webs of suffering around us—webs that we can spend thousands of dollars and years upon years trying to untangle in various types of therapy.

We've become quite accustomed to indulging the ravages of petty mind as it asserts itself through the demands of the body. We have quite lost touch with what it is that we should take action upon versus fully experience and simply hold with no other response than our presence. Werner Erhard coined the idea of "sitting like a brick" with these manifestations to describe this disposition which does not allow compromise in the form of our sitting practice, yet is fully able to open to that which arises within the boundaries of that form.

Later in this section we'll discuss some of the other supporting practices in detail. One of those is exercise, which is especially valuable in giving us the ability to train our bodies in discipline and to learn to discriminate between the decoy voices of "pain" the psyche will use to get us to back off and the authentic indications of unease that tell us we are pushing too aggressively in our work. Sometimes we simply have to give orders to the body, remind it who is in charge, and plant the flag of unwavering practice in its path. My experience in working with thousands of people in workshops and talks is that we could stand to be a little more firm with ourselves in this respect.

Regina Sara Ryan, in her book *Praying Dangerously,* writes that "Method is a straightjacket. It is meant to tie us down. It is meant to force us to find the tiny trapdoor that lies at the bottom of the soul."[1]

CHAPTER EIGHT

Sitting Practice: The Posture of the Body

In our consideration of "the posture of the body" we will include all the material details of sitting practice: how to sit, where to sit, and when to sit.

How to Sit

There are numerous "schools" or traditions of spiritual practice, and more and more appear on the scene all the time. Attendant with those traditions and their developing off-shoots are many varying recommendations about the practice of meditation—what it is and what it's for. While there are infinite and divergent forms of meditation we could discuss, the practice of sitting meditation seems to have some basic agreement cross-traditionally, with minor variations.

To engage a strong basic posture, we can sit on a cushion cross-legged (not necessarily in a lotus position) with closed eyes, mouth slightly open and jaw loose (yet breathing through the nose), spine relatively straight (but not rigid), and the hands placed in the lap. The left hand should be over the right hand with the middle joints of the middle fingers together and the thumbs lightly touching, as if holding a piece of paper between them. In this position the hands should form an oval.

In addition, we turn our head to the right just far enough that we can lightly rest our chin on our right buttock.

(Okay . . . I just wanted to see if you were paying attention —or would actually try that "in addition" part. If by any chance you did try and succeeded, do not begin a sitting practice but, instead, contact your nearest circus.)

If we are unable to sit cross-legged on the floor, we can sit upright in a chair or on a meditation bench. If possible, we should avoid leaning against anything to support the back, as an unsupported sitting posture trains the body to hold an optimal alignment of the spine throughout the day and permits a more unrestricted flow of energy in the body.

A presenter I once heard in a seminar on this subject was asked the question, "Can I meditate while lying down?" His response was, "I don't know, can you?"—his point being that most people cannot do so and remain alert, which is why lying down for meditation is not recommended unless there is absolutely no alternative due to health concerns.

Sitting on one's bed or using bedding material—pillows, sheets or blankets—for warmth or support is also not recommended. Our intention is to train the body and mind to rest consciously in a posture of wakefulness. When we use postures and objects for meditation that the mind associates with unconsciousness, we're setting up unnecessary hurdles for our practice. We move as little as possible during the meditation period. If movement becomes necessary, we move slowly and quietly to avoid breaking the continuity of our attention or distracting others if we are practicing together in a group.

Our posture, however we choose to sit, is an invocation. An invocation is a "calling down" or appeal to a particular mood and influence. What we are looking for in our sitting practice is a bodily posture that invokes nothing at all—no predominating qualities—a posture which does not lean one way or another, so to speak. If we are attentive to our posture and experiment with the subtleties of it—pulling in our chin a bit, relaxing more in the knees, lengthening the spine slightly, letting go of the tension in our shoulders—all this can make a difference in our practice.

We might think of the body as a highly sophisticated antenna. Minute adjustments in the positioning of our extremities, or the "aerials," can be the difference between channeling a live symphony from Carnegie Hall and old reruns of *Hogan's Heroes*. So we can experiment with ourselves, make modifications in the posture of our body, and watch the screen of consciousness to see what kind of reception we get. If we master this antenna called the human body/mind, we are ultimately able to host the channel that is broadcasting nothing. Channel zero. No hum, no static, no noise—simply a gloriously blank screen.

Then there is also a channel called the Surprise Channel. The Surprise Channel is the transmission station of creative intelligence. If we learn to stabilize in the clear reception of this channel, we can actually begin to feel and know what is wanted and needed by evolution itself. Our ability to receive this channel does not necessarily mean we will be able to *act* on the information we obtain in the reception of it. That's another consideration altogether, which we'll get to in the chapter on integration of spiritual experience. But we can't even receive the Surprise Channel in the first place if we're addicted to the Shopping Channel, basically the only channel to which most North Americans have access. Their antennae are permanently tuned to it. The Shopping Channel transmits from the Mind-As-Salesman Broadcasting Company and specializes in endless forms of distraction in the guise of entertainment, reruns of past personal events, hopes and dreams which have no correlating possibility in our actual lives (science fiction), and the provision of the full production services required to bring desire to a fever pitch of internal tension.

The principle of right posture is that our practice will follow our body. Gymnasts learn when performing acrobatics that the entire body follows the head. When springing off of a trampoline into the air, a performer must first throw his or her head backwards to execute a back flip, since the rest of the body follows the lead of the head. It's one of the first things gymnasts, and also dancers, learn. Where one moves attention, one moves the eyes; where the eyes go, the head goes; where the head goes, the body follows. The same is then true of the mind, which will follow the lead of the whole body. Often we can change our whole perspective by examining and instituting minor shifts in our outer form.

Before she moved, a former neighbor of ours arranged to use our address as a forwarding address for her credit card statements. Although she closed the account years ago, we're still getting statements addressed to her. It seems that when she made her last payment on the card before canceling it, she overpaid by a few cents. The company's system wouldn't treat the account as closed until she contacted them and told them where to send the credit for this final amount. She finally did this. A month later we started getting the letters again. Now the statements were showing that she owed the very amount which the company had finally paid out. I opened one of the statements and read it to her over the phone. There was only one sentence on it. It read: "You will continue to receive a statement until your balance is zero."

This is how the mind works. It continues to make irritating statements until the balance of our body is nil. We achieve this balance through attentiveness, making minor adjustments, strengthening the overall system, and abandoning ourselves into complete human embodiment. This "nil balance" is the true ground of silence.

The Zen tradition, in its practice of *zazen,* relies almost exclusively on posture as the most crucial aspect of sitting practice. Zazen practice is to sit without koans, mantras, chanting, visualization or praying; to sit without anything but oneself. In the Zen tradition the last thing we would abandon is our posture.

In *Zen Mind, Beginner's Mind,* Suzuki Roshi describes the significance of this posture.

> The most important thing in taking the zazen posture is to keep your spine straight. Your ears and your shoulders should be on one line. Relax your shoulders, and push up towards the ceiling with the back of your head. And you should pull your chin in. When your chin is tilted up, you have no strength in your posture; you are probably dreaming.[1]

> Enlightenment is not some good feeling or some particular state of mind. The state of mind that exists when you sit in the right posture is, itself, enlightenment. If you cannot be satisfied with the state of mind you have

in zazen, it means your mind is still wandering about. Our body and mind should not be wobbling or wandering about. In this posture there is no need to talk about the right state of mind. You already have it. This is the conclusion of Buddhism.[2]

But posture is often the first thing we abandon in our attempt to meditate. We allow a "floating posture" which leans and drifts, droops or bends in response to the wanderings of the mind. Zen practice is founded on the understanding of the interdependence of body and mind. Paying attention to the body through posture is how we pay attention to the mind; it is the fence that trains our attention not to stray too far from home.

Vipassana meditation practice, or insight meditation, honors a similar understanding. In Vipassana practice one watches the mind by watching all the arising sensations within the frame of the body and practicing equanimity in the presence of those feelings and sensations. Vipassana practice holds that to rest in acceptance of all arising sensations is identical to the complete acceptance of the mind, and that nothing can arise in the mind without a correlating effect within the body.

By paying attention to our posture in meditation practice we learn to fully inhabit the body that we have; we meet the moment at a visceral level, not in some conceptual, intellectual, or ethereal realm. When we take up a sitting practice and commit to right posture, we become like a greased pole which the mice of the mundane cannot climb. We hold our attention above the scurrying of the unconscious and rest in a full-feeling relationship to the body. Suzuki Roshi again advises us:

The most important point is to own your own physical body. If you slump, you will lose your self. Your mind will be wandering about somewhere else: you will not be in your body. This is not the way. We must exist right here, right now! This is the key point.[3]

To stop your mind does not mean to stop the activities of mind. It means your mind pervades your whole body.[4]

The aim is to develop one posture so that the body becomes an integrated unit, serving one master. That integration occurs by remaining still and allowing the walls that we've erected between the various parts of our psyche, and which have counterparts in the actual body, to be dismantled by the strength of our practice. If we can hold our seat with our posture, if we are willing not to run or hide from the truth of our personal underworld, each time we do so a small piece of the power and strength that is held by the forces of our unconscious is seeded over to our conscious motives and intentions—not because we have conquered anything or overpowered the untamed side of our psyches but because we have simply listened, yielded our presence to the creatures of our own darkness, and in return gained access to more of ourselves.

Ordinarily we separate the body into good parts and bad parts; useful parts and useless parts; ugly parts and beautiful parts. We sit to achieve wholeness in the body. That wholeness is not an attitude, but a simple full occupancy of the body. We do not have to do anything but be with the body as it is through our attention to posture; that alone shatters the barriers which have made us internally into a disagreeable crowd. In sitting this way we "collect" ourselves. A good solid posture is the crowd control we exact to gather ourselves up as an individual who can practice; we forge a posture for one. As the fierce and venerable Zen master Deshimaru put it, "Sit on two chairs and you will fall down. Run after two rabbits and both will escape you. You must concentrate on only one. Then one becomes all."[5]

Right posture is the center point of mind. Our thoughts orbit us as a solar system of ideas. Fragments of beliefs, preferences and prejudices are what we usually identify with and refer to as we make moment to moment decisions about how to be in our world. Usually, instead of simply becoming aware that these bits and pieces of conditioning are constantly circulating around us, we unconsciously go for a ride on them and find ourselves disoriented in some "outer space." When we take up a strong posture, we find the center of that universe, and that center point is like the hub of a carnival wheel: it is still and silent while all the rest whirls around it. As human beings we have a right to a seat at the center of that wheel; we cannot be dizzied in that seat. As Deshimaru constantly reminded his students during *sesshin,* "Don't move, don't move."

But the body wants to move us. The habits of the body which are in service to our overactive minds want us to be involved in some kind of monkey business—some entertainment, achievement or gain. Simply to remain still and present requires tremendous intention and courage. This willingness to remain still has been described by Japanese Zen master Kosho Uchiyama in his book, *Opening the Hand of Thought,* as "active participation in loss." The late Indian saint, Swami Prajnanpad, identified this condition as being "passively-active." Though we seem to be doing nothing, we are actually bringing a very intentional and dynamic presence into play that can move mountains in the realm of our internal practice.

My own teacher used the famous example of the monk who assumed a meditation posture in public, doused himself with gasoline, and then set himself on fire to protest the atrocities of the Vietnam war. When he fell over while burning, he immediately righted himself and "held his seat" as he burned to death. My teacher suggested that we should all have this kind of commitment to our form. While obviously an extreme example, the monk's actions demonstrated the extent to which a human being can become rooted in the authority of practice—an authority which, if developed, can relate to external obstacles and conflicts without having to wage war in response. This monk went to radical lengths to bring attention to the possibility of practice. Such sacrifices are usually misunderstood and made in vain, but if we are willing to acknowledge such fearlessness, even though it makes us uncomfortable, we can sometimes catch a thread of such courage ourselves.

In the future, our culture will be viewed by history as having one predominating focus and hobby: that of collecting small and petty comforts, as if a large enough stockpile of them would be the thing which could finally deliver us from our misery and suffering. This context of collecting comforts underlies even the pursuit of spiritual life in the West. The so-called spiritual practices of the New Age and other fast-food "spiritual" movements—which are absurdly and unfortunately treated as spiritual traditions—have no tradition behind them at all, only this modern Western-world phenomenon of the drive and competition for comfort, convenience, sameness and self-service.

Unfortunately, even established Eastern lineages which have found their way to North America are being slowly eroded and disempowered by the influence of Western culture; for example, the American Zen community legislating elimination of the "stick" and essentially binding the hands of authentic masters who are attempting to transmit the very essence of Zen practice—this in the name of a "civilized" approach to practice that in actuality may gut the core of the tradition itself. We may as well practice archery without arrows, the culinary arts without food.

Many of our ideas in the West about fairness, equality and independence are resting on top of attitudes that are very hazardous to a life of spiritual practice. If we allow ourselves to indulge the prevalent conventional attitude that assumes that whatever is difficult must be harmful, wrong, or an attempt to take advantage of us, then we will never develop the profound appreciation and gratitude that can eventually fire our dedication to these forms.

A friend, a long-time meditator who suffered at one point from a condition which made it impossible for her to sit, described how she came to experience just the very form, the basic posture, of meditation as the greatest luxury. "We don't know what we have until it's no longer available to us," she remarked, referring to her own lost opportunity to simply take up the posture of meditation and luxuriate in this simple but wondrous sacrament of form.

Shakespeare has used the circumstance of mistaken identity on many occasions as the basis for both tragedy and farce. Our misunderstanding of spiritual practice in the West qualifies alternately as tragic and farcical as we sacrifice traditionally-empowered forms of practice—forms which were brought here to the West after being perfected by legions of masters over thousands of years—and trade them for the calm, quiet, soft persona of "spiritual seeker" that we imagine will make us holy or conscious individuals. We miss how this kind of non-discriminating Jell-O life only hangs on a core of pride, separation, superiority and self-love. We can't see the hard rock of ego at the core of our cultural conditioning with all the layers of icing which surround it. And we can never soften at the heart unless we first learn to protect our practice through a visible discipline and outer dedication to authentic form.

To honor form this way is to exercise a specific set of practice muscles. To exercise proper posture in meditation is in some ways similar to the exercise we might perform in a gymnasium. Many of us have seen individuals in the gym who seem to be "working out" all the time. Yet somehow their strength, overall health, and well-being do not seem to improve. If we're lifting a weight to strengthen our arms but swing our body wildly to help get the weight up to our shoulder, we never strengthen the arm at all but dilute the benefit we want to realize by adopting the quickest and easiest strategy to get the apparent result. We have to know what we are exercising and isolate our efforts to that effect, directing the force of our activity toward the desired result. This requires clear intention.

If we exercise without intention, then our efforts are blunt and cannot penetrate the resiliency of the rubber balloon we live in and have mistakenly identified with as our self. This *self-sense* balloon is very cunning; its self-preservation is ensured by its seeming flexibility. When we push against it from the inside, it gives the illusion of giving way to our efforts. When it stretches to accommodate us, we come to the conclusion that we are not actually imprisoned within it, because prison walls, as everyone knows, are solid. But though it seems to be yielding, the balloon is still knotted around us; we are still captured within its confines.

Intention sharpens the point of our efforts. If the point is sharp enough, even gentle pressure with the peak of our intention on this rubber jail can cause it to explode; can shatter its ability to sustain itself. Otherwise, we may "sit" every day, or even for hours a day, thinking that we're performing some great feat, but without the incisiveness of form, we may not progress at all. In fact, if we sit, but allow our body to literally vacillate to and fro, slump into despondency, or reel in reactivity to displeasure, we can actually deepen the illusions we are hoping to confront and evaporate.

Ego only needs to be in its place—relegated to its appropriate function—not destroyed. It should be a protective shell; like nuts, fruits and vegetables have. That in us which is most valuable, the very seeds in us that can sprout and bear fruit, should be something we protect within the solid and clearly defined shell of our practice. Without such protection, whatever sweetness we may gain is immediately eaten by wild birds or dissipated by strong winds.

If instead of aligning ourselves with this kind of fierce practice and discipline we go immediately for what feels "right" and comfortable, then we never build a foundation or a structure that can weather the storms we will have to face as we journey more deeply into ourselves. With this kind of approach we may practice for many years and wind up with nothing at all in our hands. As an old saying goes, "What is sweet in the beginning is bitter in the end; what is bitter in the beginning is sweet in the end."

Osho Rajneesh puts the value of real practice in perspective in his book, *Meditation: The Art of Ecstasy.*

There are false techniques that are easier to do. They never lead you anywhere. If you are just after experiences you will fall prey to any false technique. A real technique is not concerned with experiences as such. A real technique is concerned with growth. Experiences happen; that is irrelevant. My concern is with growth, not with experiences.[6]

There is absolutely no substitute for practice. Practice is our way into posture. Posture is our way into the body. The body is the way into the heart of silence.

Where to Sit

We spoke earlier about meditation being a descent. It is not an accident that in the formal meditation practice we descend to the floor where we commit ourselves to start anew, beginning again from the ground of a solid and undeniable reality. Here we place ourselves at the level of "beginner's mind," the phrase Suzuki Roshi coined to describe the innocence and lack of pretension which characterize a successful apprenticeship to the practice of meditation.

In the simple act of sitting down, in a quiet out-of-the-way place, we make a strong statement to the unconscious. Just sitting we make the declaration that we are willing to humble ourselves; willing to accept wisdom at the level of the basics; willing to move ourselves out of being the center of attention and to receive; willing to give up our place and status in the world, even if for only an hour, and to remember that essentially we are not indispensable to any job, position or throne. We are consenting to move into the territory of the unconscious, moving down beneath the surface of things, below the level of appearances from which we normally conduct our lives, and allowing that territory to teach us, instruct us, inform us.

It is very helpful if we can establish a consistent place to sit which will offer us a refuge from our daily distractions. It is most important that we can sit without actually being interrupted, although if we are overly insistent on having it be perfectly quiet during our sitting time then our very insistence itself becomes more of a distraction than a support. The little policeman inside will jump at any opportunity to start writing out tickets to "what is," so the fewer rules, restrictions and regulations we start with the better. By sitting in the same location each time we meditate we build a momentum which allows us to stand on the shoulders of our previous efforts and to sustain our practice even in difficult times.

This principle becomes particularly active when we meditate not only in the same location but with a group of friends, like-minded or similarly motivated practitioners in the same space. To sit together, either as a family, with coworkers, or with fellow church members, has effects that extend beyond the boundaries of individual practice. A member of such a group can progress much more quickly based upon the strength of practice held by others in the group. Even though there may be no verbal or instructional exchange, a subtle exchange takes place between those who meditate together. To sit together in any kind of group builds a subtle nervous system between the practicing individuals that can be tangibly felt and utilized by those members as an energetic support for formal and daily practice. Those who meditate together in groups may experience a greater harmony or intimacy among its members. Old conflicts or patterns which may have plagued the relationship dynamics of a group in the past can dissolve and fall away over time without having to be "worked out" or confronted at the level of its symptoms.

We may want to enhance the sanctuary of our sitting space with a few artifacts or invocational objects. Candles, flowers, incense, a picture of a saint or spiritual master or, of course, our own teacher if we have one are all commonly used empowerments for a sitting space. The important thing is that our sitting area doesn't become cluttered, that we do not allow the already vacillating and fleeting nature of our mind to do the decorating in our sitting area and wind up with an external manifestation of the confused mind that is within us on an altar before us. Again, the space itself should be invocational. It should serve as a tangible reminder and resting point for the simplicity of ordinary and open awareness. If we're not careful we can turn our sitting space into a shopping mall of spiritual options and bewilder ourselves instead of creating refuge for our practice.

Just as our actual posture should help us to become "one" person, with one whole and integrated body, so should our sitting space help us to meet ourselves where we are. The difficulty is that where we are is buried underneath a mound of distractions, and so we have to dig deep down to meet ourselves in the moment. If our sitting space has artifacts from a dozen different traditions and pictures of several masters, all of whom we claim as our own teacher, it's as if we are trying to hit water by digging a dozen wells that are ten feet deep and digging still more shallow holes when we fail to reach the thing that would quench our thirst.

The place we sit for formal practice should be protected from the influences we have to juggle in daily life while at the same time not becoming a rigidly controlled or artificially isolated environment. For example, it is recommended in our tradition not to sit in the dark, but to have the room be well lit so that we do not begin to feel that we have to be in the dark to rest in a conscious relationship to ourselves. This is the reason why the Vipassana tradition as taught by S. N. Goenka is opposed to slow walking or slow eating practices and the modification of ordinary activity in order to be more "aware." We must develop our awareness within the realm of our ordinary activity and lives. Formal practice is designed to give us enough room to get an anchor down with respect to our capacity for presence, but it should not become a crutch; it is rather a bridge which we regularly use to cross over into ordinary conscious life.

When to Sit

Just as it is helpful to establish a regular place for meditation, so it is valuable to establish a regular hour and consistent length if possible. The most important aspect of the "when" of meditation is that we follow through with the commitment we make to our meditation routine. If we decide to meditate every day, we should not allow ourselves to miss our practice time by justifying the mind's resistance with the ever-present and inexhaustible demands of Western life.

So follow-through is extremely important. When we follow through with our plan to practice, we establish a track record in relationship to our unconscious habits; our credit improves every time we make a payment on time, and in this way we are gradually able to command a greater amount of authority and respect from the unruly characters who are always partying in our house, disrupting our overtures toward practice. Eventually these characters come to know that we mean business if we follow through consistently, and then they put up less of a fight. Consistency is the trade secret of successful meditators. That's bad news for our habitual indulgences. (The good news, however, is that consistency is only crucial for the first ten to fifteen years or so.)

Many meditators enjoy sitting early in the morning, just after waking. For many people this is a matter of practicality; it is simply the only time of day that some of us can grab an uninterrupted period for practice. No matter what is happening in our daily lives, we can always wake up a little bit earlier and take that time to sit. While it takes quite a strong intention to establish this habit, once in place we will cherish this first corner of the day; we will come to appreciate the preciousness of it.

I was traveling once with my teacher when I overheard an exchange he had with a participant in the seminar he was giving. The man had mentioned something about the demand of the schedule and how tired he was. My teacher remarked, "Well . . . you can always rest, but an opportunity may never come again." I recall his words frequently and have come to feel this way about every chance I get to practice meditation formally. Zen master Suzuki Roshi had his own personal way of handling the tendency of the mind to derail the intention to practice. He made a habit of leaping out of bed the moment he came to consciousness in the morning, before he even had the chance to think about how he felt or whether or not he was going to choose to get up for practice.

Another reason for sitting in the early morning is that many spiritual traditions identify the hours between nighttime and sunrise as being particularly advantageous for meditation. It is a time of transition, a crack between the worlds of the conscious and the unconscious. It is at this time that we are just awake enough to break free from sleep while simultaneously having some distance between ourselves and

the conventional concerns that usually dog us in the main-
stream hours. This period, the dawning of the day, has been
host to the discovery of "free moment" for many meditators.

If we can sit for an hour at a time, that's a good length for
our meditation session, though to practice for shorter periods of time is without question better than nothing at all. We
might spend that hour doing nothing more than sorting
through the stack of anxieties and preoccupations that throw
themselves at our feet when once we reach the pillow and
take up the posture, meeting each of these concerns and allowing them to subside in the wake of our attentiveness.
Often we may spend the entire hour feeling like a clerk in
the complaint department, playing host and good listener to
grievance after grievance. Whether the time passes in this
way or as an experience of having our feet up on the desk
with nothing to do but enjoy the view from our corner office
makes no difference, however. An hour is enough time if we
are practicing daily to continually deepen the quality of our
meditation. Every minute of that hour should feel sacred to
us. I have found in my own practice that it is often in the last
minutes of meditation that important openings appear and
pivotal unveilings occur. Deshimaru counsels,

> Patience.
> These last moments in zazen are very important.
> The last five minutes.
> The last minute.[7]

Having detailed what seem to be some of the most helpful aspects of form and posture, we must also acknowledge
that we often find ourselves in less than ideal conditions for
meditation. I spent almost a decade in my twenties traveling
all over the world for work and pleasure. Because my sitting

practice was a priority, I meditated anywhere I could. I've sat in sweltering tents in Australia, in my car on deserted highways in North America, in closets and bathtubs in hostels and hotels, under desks, in garages and storage rooms, in airport chapels, in barns, on boats and planes. Wherever I was, I always found a place to meditate in private each day.

A woman I recently met at a seminar told me that she arises every morning to meditate before her husband awakes. Each morning she sets up her altar space, puts out her cushion, hangs her pictures and sits. And each day she puts it all away again at the end of her practice session so as not to cause distress to her spouse, who is uncomfortable with even the idea of meditation. This woman instinctively understands the importance of not flaunting her practice. If we hold our meditation up as a challenge to others or as a way of trying to become special in the eyes of others, then we are not meditating, not letting go at all. We should meditate in private, with others who share our practice, or otherwise skillfully mask the outer form of our practice in any situation in which it would draw unnecessary attention, discussion or questions from others.

In the end, how, where and when we sit are secondary to the imperative that we sit, however we can, whenever we can. Perhaps we are ill and cannot even leave our bed and must sit propped up against a pillow to meditate. Maybe our back is weak and we have to use a particular chair from time to time. If we can only carve out twenty minutes in the privacy of our office during lunch, then this is what we have to work with in the beginning. Once we've rooted into place the habit of actually and physically sitting, then we can add those parameters that we know will benefit us, we can adjust our habits to eventually align with the supremacy of form. Bit by bit we can honor and integrate those details that can make our sitting practice more potent.

We have touched in this chapter on the merest superficialities of form. There are tomes of sacred teachings and reams of spiritual literature in many traditions that detail the importance of what we have barely grazed. Yet it is our experience and our own lived relationship to the brilliance of actual practice that are necessary if we wish to progress along the path.

CHAPTER NINE

Contextual Practice: The Posture of the Mind

Just as we intentionally position our bodies in relationship to the earth—to solid ground—we also practice the intentional alignment of our mind to the principles of right thinking. We could call right thinking "transparent thinking" —a use of the thought process which clarifies and provides a window onto that which is real, rather than a thinking that obscures, clouds or distorts that view. This is the posture of mind we practice in meditation.

It's obvious that if we want to bring our physical posture into alignment with an alternative form, we first have to examine our current posture, isolate the discrepancies between it and the desired form, and make the necessary adjustments. The same process must be engaged with the mind, although with somewhat more difficulty, since the domain of mind is much more subtle than the domain of the body. It is easier for the mind to convince us that it is oriented toward a particular principle when, in fact, there are often layers of delusion or confusion which obfuscate its *actual* orientation. Perhaps we've experienced the disorientation that results from getting feedback from others that does not fit with our idea of ourselves. It may be pointed out that our actions do not support the lip service we pay to certain principles, spiritual or otherwise.

For this reason it's important that we have a good look at the mind; make ourselves familiar with its nature. To put it bluntly, most of us are very naïve when it comes to understanding the tendencies of our untrained minds. We think everything is fine and dandy and are content to allow our mind, in its current orientation, to continue to gather data, filter that data according to its biases, and then to manage and dictate our responses without our conscious participation.

In the next breath, we are down on ourselves for our shortcomings—for our lack of control over certain behaviors; for our inability to manage our anger or find intimacy in relationship or to act in accordance with our deepest wishes. In the practice of meditation we stop browbeating *ourselves* and take a deeper look at the mechanics of the mind that should be serving us but is instead punching a clock for our unconscious habits and motives.

It's not that we begin to blame our mind, however. In meditation, this habit of finding fault is overridden or subsumed by the practice of simple observation. And the more enthusiastically we observe, the better!

How to Observe

Our job in the sanctuary of formal sitting practice is to assume the posture of the body and then to simply observe whatever arises in our conscious awareness. The posture of the mind in formal meditation is an orientation of allowance. We do not predetermine a direction for our attention. We are not "focusing" on the breath, a particular visualization, or a mantra. We are not seeking particular thoughts, feelings, experiences, the revelation of great ideas or tremendous sensations. We are not trying to stay with any one thing and "concentrate." We are opening our attention to wherever it is that attention naturally goes, and attending this movement of attention with the active participation of our awareness. That's all.

The Wings of Surrender

While the discipline of form might be called the root of meditation, the mood of surrender is its wings. In principle, meditation is about becoming present with ourselves, and eventually with all of life-as-it-is, in the moment. We've all heard this many times, of course. Bringing one's attention to the moment is quite simple in theory and a lovely principle to consider. It is, however, very difficult to practice, given our habits of attention. The truth is, because it seems so simple many of us imagine we're already living "in the moment"— perhaps even justifying our lack of commitment and willingness to take on responsibility by thinking that we are being "spontaneous."

In actuality, we cannot imagine the extraordinary and marvelous results that would ensue from actually performing the practice of meditation, both formally and informally, with the enthusiasm, vigor and passion it deserves. To simply surrender to "what is" in meditation brings us face to face with the great mystery itself, with the heart of all spiritual traditions, with the yawning miracle of creation. Though the practice has been freely shared and disseminated throughout human history in many living traditions, it remains for the most part a secret.

This is simply because the mind will take on an attractive idea or concept as happily as the newest style in shoes. The mind may even allow those ideas to lead us right to the threshold of actual practice, but when our sense of self sees the shoes of reality elegantly lined up outside of the door of practice, it balks and resists entering. This is because the door of practice leads into a hall of wonder, and the identity we don't want to give up does not want to enter the hall of wonder. In the hall of wonder the mind is helpless to do anything but wonder what it is, where it is, and even *if* it is. Eventually, a wonder-full mind is no mind at all—and that is a frightening proposition.

With our internal commitment to illusion firmly in place, the very cells in our body take on a tension that comes from the psychic activity that perpetuates ego.

One purpose of meditation is to allow each cell to shed the stress of this unnecessary tension and detoxify itself, which allows the human body to function naturally based on the integrity of its organic nature. When this psychic stress is constant, and there is no opportunity for each cell to reclaim its neutral and perfectly functioning state, those cells eventually mutate to accommodate the applied stress. Fortunately, to achieve the mutation of a cell from exposure to stress requires a long period of repeated low-level, or less enduring, exposure to very traumatic and high-level stress. Unfortunately, this is the exact circumstance under which many people are subjected to psychically toxic environments, either as children growing up in a dysfunctional or abusive family, as mates of partners who exude such toxicity, or in work environments which maintain a negative atmosphere.

It is obvious that children, at least mostly if not wholly, are innocent of choosing to subject themselves to such stress, but once bombarded in sustained fashion with such negativity, the adapted cells develop a conditioned preference to environments which feature such dysfunctional elements. So though being in relationship with a psychically unhealthy mate is something that no one who suffers such a relationship would say they want, their very cells comprise a collective dedication to perpetuating the stressful circumstances to which their cellular makeup adapted in early life. So childhood stress makes "choosing" relationship stress more probable, and relationship stress makes "choosing" career stress even more likely, and so on, until, if left to the unconscious, every facet of one's life has been selected to honor the specialized, mutated capabilities of the dis-eased cells. Once a cell has mutated, it's extremely difficult to "mutate" it back.

Regular meditation, if practiced properly over a long period of time, can unveil for the practitioner the secret of how to directly care for the cellular integrity of his or her body and how to master the ability to release stored stress from the cells at will. Eventually, one is able to release all stress related to the conceptual and intellectual faculties of the mind and completely surrender each and every cell over to the spontaneous creative intelligence of evolution, at which point each cell is discovered to be endowed with God-mind, an intelligence which surpasses all possibility present within the thinking brain-mind. If this is done, then the entire body begins to function as a unified representative of divine intelligence, and evolution can be directly served and sustained by the one who has bodily surrendered in this way to the evolutionary process.

In his childhood, the controversial Indian spiritual master Osho Rajneesh made a habit of throwing himself into the

Ganges during monsoon season when whirlpools were abundant. Upon entering one of these whirlpools, rather than fighting with the undertow, he would cooperate with it and let it drag him under without struggle. In this manner, he learned that he would always be spit out at the bottom of the water funnel, which diminished in size as he allowed himself to be drawn into it.

Similarly, to practice meditation we follow the mind and let it swirl us around and around, just going with it as it arises. We surrender to this whirlpool at the surface and let it take us in circles and begin to draw us under, down into its depths. We may think we are going to drown if we don't somehow take control of our mind, but that is the crucial moment. Instead of fighting against the movement of phenomena as they occur in the mind, we offer no resistance and only follow this whirlpool of self-concern closer and closer to its source, until the mind itself effortlessly leads us to its very point of arising. When we reach that point, if we let the mind take us there, we are automatically released from it— not through effort, but through nonreactivity.

At its origin, mind cannot hold us. What we truly are is too big. The essentially uncontainable nature of consciousness is too immense for mind if we will meet it at the point of its arising. That point has no power. Only the most superficial extremities of mind and appearances have any power, and then only temporarily, unless we fight and resist and deny what mind actually is. If we resist, then it can hold us in its grip and keep us spinning in whirlpools of illusion indefinitely.

The divine can only enter through the door of the moment. But this door in us is often locked by our commitment to our ideas about ourselves, about spirituality, about happiness or fulfillment; by our search for the sensational. Since we do not let the ordinary moment in, we also keep the divine itself locked out. When we let the moment in and the "extraordinary" stops pulling constantly on our attention, enough free attention is liberated to notice life itself, which has actually been present *all the time*. It was present even in the beginning when we began seeking it in some form of spiritual journey, the "success" of which is always nothing but a surrendering to what is ordinarily present as the natural circumstance of human life and a resting in human life to the extent that the divine becomes known and apparent.

Presence in Principle

We could say that presence is the spontaneous activity of true meditation; an activity which arises naturally in the absence of commentary, or at least in the absence of *identification* with the commentary that the mind produces in relationship to our experience.

To become present is not technically something we *do*, even though we may refer to it as the *practice* of presence. In order for presence to occur in our vicinity, or in what we might call our conscious awareness, we more accurately have to duck, dodge and artfully sidestep the ordinary cat fight which our untrained mind goads us into almost constantly, either in formal meditation itself or throughout the day. If we learn the art or knack of this stepping aside, much the way we would be trained in an aikido class to use the opponent's own force to expedite a quick exit for our enemy, then suddenly, one day, we will find presence *happening*.

Presence is simply the activity of cognition—undressed. Somewhere along the way a popular joke ended with the punch line, "I didn't recognize you with your clothes on," and it stuck. It applies here. Our perception of reality is normally all "dressed up." Attended by a battery of mental modifications, qualifiers and conditioners which grab any particular experience, thought or perception by the lapels as soon it walks through the door of awareness and before you can say, "Bob's not my uncle," that particular instant has been washed, permed, colored, kinked, manicured, leg-waxed and decked out to the nines. The thing is, this process happens so quickly—the mind is so proficient at window dressing the naked present moment—that we are not even aware this goes on. So even though each moment is getting customized and accessorized according to our tastes and wishes, we're always reeling a little—we always feel a little off balance, even if we're just out for a walk in nature. Our mind so clutters the "nature" of things *as they are* that neither the mind nor the body are any longer able to rest, or be with life *as it is.* We feel such unrest as agitation, stress, irritability, confusion, overwhelm, distraction and maybe even anxiety.

The practice of presence is designed to dissolve or evaporate this dynamic. The practice of presence is sort of an anti-practice in which, rather than doing something new, we stop doing the old thing and let what is naturally present in the absence of that habit *arise.* Presence is what would arise if we pulled the plug on the association/assumption machine. *Presence* is the marriage of the *present* to our own *absence* of interpretations. This present-absence leaves us available to see that reality, in this moment, is "just so," without the steamroller of "I" coming up from behind everything and flattening it out in relationship only to itself. Things would just appear as they are, floating in life-as-it-is, unattended by the concept that they are located in relationship to us, that they have meaning to us either as a threat or as the potential for profit. They just are.

The presence of conscious awareness and the entertainment of a separate sense of "I" are exact opposites. The only time we get into trouble is when we abandon the awareness of what "just is" and allow our conditioned perceptions of self and reality to mechanically paste on top of life all our notions and illusions about our personal individual existence.

Presence represents the simplification of perceived reality that is required in order to awaken. Normally we cake on this thing called an "ego sense" over and on top of the present moment. This creates a dynamic in which "what is" is interpreted relative to this thing we call "I" (which doesn't exist), and our separation is reinforced through the distortion we nurture. We pretend there is someone there who exists apart from all of what "just is" and then assess what impact this interpretation will have upon this illusory creature we take ourselves to be, that exists somewhere (we don't really know where), at some time (we don't really know when)—and then either find "happiness" or misery in our perception.

This is the one and only thing we have control over: whether or not we allow the habit of thinking and imagining our separate selves into existence to dominate over simply withdrawing the root of the illusion in such a way that the tree of misery falls over by itself. It is actually quite simple to do, but in our misunderstanding it's the last option that occurs to us.

The Practice of Presence in Daily Life

At first when we begin practicing meditation we rely quite heavily on the formal sitting period. As our practice deepens it eventually becomes clear that the formal sitting practice is designed to catalyze a process—a movement of attention— that is available to us at all times as the essence of practice itself. Once we develop a direct relationship to this movement of attention we are no longer dependent upon the actual period of sitting for this shift of awareness to occur. Finally, we are able to apply this movement of attention to all that we experience, feel, think or relate to as a human being. Anything that arises in the realm of our feeling and sensational experience is fair game for the application of presence. The meditative condition becomes a homing device that is constantly referencing the existence of any perceived phenomenon against the reality of impermanence. Meditation allows us to remember that both our ignorance and our enlightenment are changing and insubstantial conditions. This establishes context.

The word "presence" helps us overcome some of the standard connotations that ride on the word "meditation" so that we can escape the gravitational pull of our misunderstandings about the practice of meditation itself. For instance, we probably could not conceive of "meditating" all the time or all day long, chiefly because "meditation" has become associated for us with the qualities of peace, quiet, inactivity, and perhaps bliss. If we suggested to most any Westerner that he or she try to remain in a meditative state throughout the day, we would probably find that person slow walking, deep breathing, and talking slowly, softly and calmly. If the person were a practicing Zen Buddhist, they would most likely make the translation to their own practice of mindfulness. Mindfulness practice, however, also carries some of the same baggage as the word "meditation" does for us in the West and was "invented" in another cultural matrix, at another time, for a distinct clientele who ain't us.

We could call the practice of presence a "meditative stance" —that is, we take the piercing nature of yielding awareness that we discover in our sitting practice into our daily lives and continue to assert this awareness with open eyes, open mouths and active limbs. In the midst of our activity we keep one eye on our work in the world—our relationships, our responsibilities—while simultaneously committing toward all facets of that activity the recognition that "it is simply so." We encircle our experience, our arising needs, the objects, people and circumstances with whom we come into contact with this "just-so-ness." While intelligently moving each of these things forward with one hand as needed, we hold them and stroke them with the other hand. This second hand represents our appreciation, our recognition of each manifestation's or condition's simple existence. Its "is-ness" is given the warmth of our gently pressing regard.

The practice of presence is a soft, yet piercing, attention. Its lack of aggressiveness and radical receptivity allow everything to enter its gaze. This can only be done through a tacit relationship to the body. The mind, by itself, is only capable of concentration, a condition in which we usually limit rather than expand our attention, project a perceived need or outcome into the future, and then attempt to achieve it. Presence, which requires a relaxation of the mind's habitual narrowing, arises naturally when the body opens as a whole to that which is presently arising. Our mind is a part of this whole body and is part of the relaxation. Just as we would train our bodies to delay gratification for the purpose of maturing in form, we train our minds to delay interpretation so that we may mature in spirit. This delay creates a gap in which, before the mind has an opportunity to draw conclusions about what it is witnessing, consciousness has moved on to a deeper level of receptivity from which it continues to embrace further evidence that everything that is *is simply present*—exempt from labeling, categorizing and ranking for ranking's sake. Critical judgment will be allowed to deploy itself when the practice of presence naturally allows discrimination based on the needs of the moment.

This natural allowance or recognition of differences within the context of radical acceptance is the open attitude with which we embrace all things without judgment. Simultaneously, we allow that they have a distinct place in the world, with an appropriately corresponding value; not value from the standpoint of worth, but from the perspective of purpose. When we allow things to have their purpose without saddling them with any degree of rank, we achieve true relationship.

Presence is an attention that is both penetrating and diffuse. It remains with what is real, but being nonaggressive, it does not try to control or manipulate the features of reality toward which it naturally turns. Wherever that attention goes, there the quality of acceptance and expansiveness is represented and applied without hesitation to whatever manifestations want to shake hands with it or have their babies kissed by it, even though it is devoid of political motive. In fact, we could call presence "embrace without motive."

Presence as an Active Assertion

Two boys who often played together would sometimes challenge the younger children in the neighborhood to keep up with them, running ahead into a nearby wood. When the smaller children followed, they routinely led them to a creek that was just narrow enough for the older boys to jump but just wide enough that the younger children would be stopped short.

One day a small boy who was new to the neighborhood took up the pursuit. Upon reaching the creek, instead of abandoning the chase as expected, he paused and studied the distance spanned by the stream. Then, with calculated intent, the boy backed up several steps from the bank and leaped purposefully into the middle of the water. Landing once in the very center of the creek, the boy planted his foot with unhesitating assertiveness. The impact of the sole of his shoe perfectly displaced the eight inches of water beneath it to clear an open step right to the graveled bottom of the creek. From there he took a second jump which delivered him unstained and utterly dry onto the opposite bank where the older, and now speechless, boys waited.

In similar fashion, it is the impact that our asserted presence has in the stream of the present moment that clears away the flood of misperceptions and anguished concerns that normally inundate and soil us. It is this presence of awareness, the undivided commitment of our attention to "what is," that allows us to enter every moment with a force of being that repels the waters of petty mind; and that allows us to depart from that moment before becoming soaked through by the dullness of perception which renders even the extraordinary mundane. As spiritual teacher Arnaud Desjardins has put it in his book by the same title, we must "jump into life."

The essence of the practice of presence is to simply remember that reality "is what it is" in the present moment and to actively place our attention upon that reality with such passion that there is no more room for the mind's habit of interpretation to steal to the throne where only our presence ought to rule. And indeed, we must assert this awareness again and again over a long period of time before the old habits of mind begin to weaken and wane under the influence of practice.

Few practitioners have the requisite longing and desire to know reality this way, however. Most of us are constantly

Taisen Deshimaru

Deshimaru founded the Zen Temple of La Gendronniere, France, the largest Zen dojo in the West. With his students he founded more than one hundred dojos in Europe. At the death of his master, Deshimaru remained sitting in zazen for forty-nine days.

Suzuki Roshi

Shogaku Shunryu Suzuki Roshi, Soto Zen master, was a founding father of the American Zen community and the author of the spiritual classic, *Zen Mind, Beginner's Mind.* He founded the San Francisco Zen Center and Buddhist monastery Tassajara, Zen Mountain Center.

Photo courtesy of San Francisco Zen Center.

Chögyam Trungpa Rinpoche

Chögyam Trungpa Rinpoche was one of the most dynamic teachers of Buddhism in the twentieth century. This photo, taken in 1971, is from a gathering at 4 Mile Canyon House in Boulder, Colorado, Chögyam Trungpa Rinpoche's residence at the time.

Photo courtesy of Shambhala Publishing & Archives.

Lee Lozowick

Lee Lozowick is a contemporary spiritual master, author,
and spiritual son of the late Indian saint, Yogi Ramsuratkumar.

Photo provided by Hohm Press.

Irina Tweedie

Born in Russia in 1907, Mrs. Tweedie became the lineage holder
to her Sufi master, whom she called Bhai Sahib, through an
arduous process of spiritual purification and training. Her journey
is chronicled in the spiritual classic *Daughter of Fire.* The work of
her master continues through Llewellyn Vaughan-Lee and The
Golden Sufi Center, P.O. Box 428, Inverness, CA 94937-0428,
U.S.A. E-mail GoldenSufi@aol.com.

Photo courtesy of The Golden Sufi Center.

diving headlong into torrid love affairs with our own cherished belief systems, superimposing them onto the pristine panorama of reality like a bad artist who covers over a Renoir with his own undisciplined version of art.

Desperately seeking satisfaction in the arms of interpretation, we miss the embrace of the divine.

The Labyrinth of Illusion

Presence as a practice involves our reaching out and putting our hand on "what is," anchoring our attention upon that which is real and asserting that in every moment.

When carnivals used to travel with fun house mazes, a hall of mirrors into which fair-goers could enter and enjoy the temporary fun of becoming snared in a labyrinth of dead ends and false beginnings, people would often wander for long periods, eventually being forced to abandon their effort to reach the exit.

But there is a practical secret to the completion of these mazes which quite accurately depicts the practice of presence. If upon entering one puts his or her hand on one wall (or on that which is real) and does not remove that hand but only continues to walk, following the line of unbroken continuity of any tangible wall, he or she will eventually, lawfully, and without fail reach the end of the labyrinth and walk out the other side. One may be led to the turnaround point of any number of dead ends, but once having explored a false trail by this method, one will never enter that particular cul-de-sac again. In similar manner, if we put our attention on what is real and remain fixed upon it, we are guaranteed to be delivered beyond the labyrinth of our illusions into reality.

If, however, we enter into the fun house maze and trust what "appears to be" to our eyes, we can become indefinitely delayed in an endless loop of misinterpretation and misperception. When we are with what is real and we use the meditative practice as our guide, we are no longer in need of *any* interpretation to live, to progress, or to evolve. We are then safely guided by the reliability of "what is" itself.

Eventually, we come to the understanding that to be with "what is" is so reliable that the only reason we would choose not to remain with "what is" is that ego does not want to be delivered out of the illusion. It wants to remain tricked. It wants to remain in the hall of mirrors where it can endlessly gaze at itself and be led further into dead-end situations where there is nothing to do but reflect upon its own image —nothing to do but contemplate (through endless forms of speculation) the existence of itself and enjoy the comfort and safety (for ego) of being lost, separate, and apparently individual.

The Lion of Reality

The willingness to make use of and consider the practice of presence requires that we reconnect to the part of ourselves which remembers and longs for the essentially limitless and boundless nature of the Self. Most of us, however, have been driven brutally away from the delicacy and sublimity of "what is" by ignorant adults who, separated from acknowledgement of the divine themselves, did not realize what they were doing. To muster the willingness, courage or appetite to knock on the door of reality requires that we update our condition and realize that we are not the fragile and delicate children that were shamed or abandoned long ago. If we reopen our longing for the very mystery that human life makes it possible to engage, that longing will eventually draw forth secrets that will sing an open symphony of understanding and communion to our heart. But it takes great persistence to get the universe to open up its arms and make available its magic.

Reality is like a great, lazy, sleeping lion who sits motionless with closed eyes in the sun at the city zoo. Most of us are like those who crowd around the edges of the cage, taking pictures of the beast outside of his natural habitat and discussing how regal he is from the safety of our contrived relationship to truth, never confronting the terror that would arise in us if we ever met "what is" face to face in real life. We are satisfied and content to be spiritual tourists, gawking at life through fences.

If we are serious about having a relationship to reality, then such a visit to the cage of spiritual concepts will never satisfy us. But the environment of the zoo does not call forth from the lion of reality the qualities that make it supreme master of the jungle. So we have to sneak into the lion's cage, crawl over the barbed wire of socially acceptable ideas and action, and make like a lion cub, playing around the feet of the present moment, doing our best to get its attention. We start tackling its legs, nipping at its tail and jumping on its back. Mostly it just gently moves us aside, shakes us easily from its fur, casually ignores our childish attempts to get it to engage.

But if we continue to exercise the practice of presence and formal meditation, then we get bigger and stronger and become more noticeable to the lion of reality, not as easy to brush aside. If we persist and bother it enough, never content with just a fleeting glance in our direction, then one day the lion of life gets provoked by our unrelenting presence and insistence upon a response and it unleashes the full ferocity of its regard, roars its mighty call of grace, and deafens us forever to the noise of the mundane world.

Presence Is Only Human

The principles and practice of basic meditation must be grappled with for some time before presence can be reliably established in daily life. The highest function of our abiding presence is to feed the divine, or evolution, itself. By using our feeling attention and directing it toward or opening it to "what is," the thing our attention is on is divinized and feeds the heart of divine communion.

The heart of divine communion is like a raging furnace: brilliant white hot—so hot that its radiance literally allows for the possibility of all life. But in order for the furnace to exist and keep burning, it must be fed. When we enter onto the path of practice or step into a lineage, we are agreeing to a very specific use of our presence. Our presence then becomes like a shovel. Everything that exists in the world, anything that *is*, is just coal: an organic substance which has energy bound up in its structure. When we're practicing presence—or allowing it, surrendering to it—we're using our attention to go get the coal and put it in the furnace. This process in which we surrender our attention to "what is" is how we feed the divine.

By taking this meditative stance, a stance that assigns one foot to a place in the world and the other to an anchor in the furnace, we develop a facility in both domains of existence. When we are able to function in the world while simultaneously keeping one eye on the furnace, the heart of communion, then the divine is fed by what exists in the world and can use that food to serve its evolutionary needs.

Only a human being can do this for the divine. *Presence is only human.*

CHAPTER TEN

Supporting Practices: The Posture of Lifestyle

The Integration Equation

By practicing the posture of the body and the posture of the mind, we become vulnerable to the obviousness of union, available to the glory of emptiness, receptive to the majesty of mind—pure and open. These first two postures are revelatory in nature; they support the revelation of true freedom. But revelation needs a partner if we want to truly progress on the path without unnecessary setbacks, obstacles and hindrances. That partner is integration.

It is perfectly possible to access tremendous degrees of revelation just by accident, even if we are not practicing at all. In fact, some people, like the brilliant and controversial R. D. Laing, for instance, calculate that psychiatric hospitals are full of such individuals. The difference between revelation being the source of a tremendous instability that may cause the breakdown of an individual's ability to function and the same revelation being the catalyst for liberation in daily life depends upon the practitioner's ability to integrate the radically new point of view. If we looked at it from a mathematical standpoint, we could say that revelation multiplied by integration equals the net value of our practice.

If we have fifty revelations but by the time we stop bouncing off the walls, seeing lights, hosting visions or cavorting with mystical deities we are able to integrate only one of them into an ordinary kindness, then the product of our practice is one. If, on the other hand, we have only one revelation but can successfully make use of that revelation in every corner of our waking lives, then the value of our practice is unlimited and will continue to grow in each moment we participate fully in our lives and in the lives of others.

If we conducted a research study on all those who have been lottery winners in the history of North America, I suspect we would find that winning the lottery is absolutely no guarantee of becoming a wealthy person. In fact, we could probably locate a person who had won $10,000 and through a series of investments and wise decisions was able to grow that money into assets sufficient to last a lifetime and to pass something on to future generations as well. On the other hand, we could find individuals who have won millions of dollars, yet somehow, within months, have wound up empty-handed and destitute. It is exactly the same in the domain of spiritual energy and spiritual experience. We have to be educated on how to invest and make use of what we get. In fact, most of us would be lucky if a great insight lasted more than a few seconds, much less a lifetime.

The supporting practices—the posture of lifestyle—are the means by which we prepare ourselves to integrate revelation, spiritual experience and the potent energies to which we can suddenly gain access through our practice of meditation. As the old saying goes, the wise prepare for war in peacetime, or, as the well-known financial advisor Howard Ruff put it, "It wasn't raining when Noah built the ark." We strengthen the posture of lifestyle in anticipation of igniting a vitality we may have been suppressing since childhood, or of arousing the serpent of *kundalini,* the famous life force of awakening that can unleash itself in the body.

We may scoff at the idea that there are radical energy phenomena that can be catalyzed into play within the body if we have never experienced such a thing ourselves. We may think that those who do report such experiences are making it up to satisfy their need to be special or entertain themselves. But many ancient spiritual traditions were well aware of the dangers involved in experimenting with consciousness, with deeply examining the connection between the human body and mind, and these traditions went to great lengths to devise methods of protection which would allow spiritual practitioners to ride on the wave of an internally awakened life force instead of suffering permanent damage to the nervous system or losing one's mind in the radical groundlessness which opens in realization.

That's the extreme end of the spectrum. At a more mundane level the reason we engage the posture of lifestyle is simply to avoid unconsciously wasting the energies we might gain from formal sitting practice. The saying "A chain is only as good as its weakest link" certainly holds true in the domain of spiritual practice. If we are able to rouse a powerful inner force through the contemplative practice of meditation but have a weakness and lack of discipline around our habits of sexual interaction, for example, then the energy we gain in formal sitting gets immediately "spent" as soon as we're back on two

feet and our unconscious habit has the use of our legs to mo-
bilize itself. We spend that energy on the conquest of sexual
partners or, more subtly, in the compulsive need to attract others' attention, women and/or men, by flirting, strutting or pos-
turing in some way. Then we're like a pot smoker who appears
to be very blissful and loving but cannot be relied upon to do
the shopping because they're so hungry they blow the entire
month's food budget on one trip to the supermarket.

The basic methods by which one can gain strength and
stability in the body and mind are cross-traditional. Many different spiritual schools, through their own experimentation,
have independently come to similar conclusions with respect
to the means by which revelation can be sustained and spiritual experience successfully integrated. These methods deal
with five basic aspects of lifestyle: the diet of the mind, the
diet of the body, exercise of the body, work of the body, and
the management of sexual energy in the body. In my own tradition, we refer to these as the practices of study, exercise,
diet, right livelihood, and monogamous relationship.

Recognizing Pregnancy

In addition to the strength of protection these lifestyle practices
can afford, they have another function, which is to harmonize
the psychophysical apparatus into a condition from which we
can more easily sense the subtle and refined energies of spirit
that will seem invisible or nonexistent to us if we are host to
sensations which are volatile, heightened, and unrelenting.

A medical nurse described to a friend of mine how a
woman was brought into the emergency room complaining
of severe stomach pains. The woman was vastly overweight,
and within a short amount of time the hospital staff determined that she was about to give birth and they informed

her so. "But I'm not pregnant," the woman argued, even as she proceeded to go into labor. Although such a circumstance is hard to imagine, we're all in a similar condition spiritually. Even when we're told by the saints and other midwives of consciousness that we're pregnant with spirit, like the woman in the hospital, we're so "overweight" with distraction that we deny it. Once we increase our sensitivity and awareness, however, we find ourselves unable to fathom how we could have overlooked what was true all along.

We can increase our sensitivity by turning up our awareness or by turning down the distraction. If the volume of our stereo system is drowning out the birdsong in our backyard, we obviously have to turn the stereo down to enjoy it, not petition the birds to chirp up a little. The extra "weight" on our attention that we're unnecessarily carrying around distracts us from the obvious truth. The lifestyle recommendations are for this purpose: to turn down the volume of distraction that keeps us from deep meditation and unwavering presence.

A style of Vipassana that was brought to the West by S. N. Goenka employs the analogy of an off-shore oil rig in poor weather to describe the need to manage our sensations. The only time the crew can drill for oil is when the sea is calm. If a storm is raging and large waves are pounding the rig, all work stops. There is no retrieval of the valued resource under such circumstances. The same is true in the body and mind. If our sensations are raging on the surface, we can hardly tune in to the deeper currents of awareness that can reveal to us the clarity we desire.

The Diamond of Presence

In short, we meditate, practice presence in daily life, study, eat well, exercise, mate and work rightly. As we mature, the ways in which we protect and nurture our practice extend far beyond these basic conditions and ultimately reach into absolutely every thread of our lives. For now, however, imagine these six activities practiced thoroughly; meaning that everything we do in the world is accompanied by the context or mood of one or more of them.

For instance, if we have to take the bus across town to get to work, we either read something which has value from a perspective of right thinking (like the allegorical novels of C. S. Lewis rather than the *National Enquirer*) or we observe ourselves and others on the bus in a way that deepens our ability to make clear distinctions about our condition or the condition of humans in general. If we're doing that, we are effectively "studying." When we weave one or the other of the lifestyle practices into our ordinary life activities, these practices, or tangent points to presence, begin to develop potency. The more diligently the postures of lifestyle are assumed, the more tightly they band around us and the more protection and strength we are afforded. This creates a kind of sealed chamber, inside of which the magnetism of our intention to honor and cherish these postures keeps this chamber charged with a daring lack of options and distractions from reality as it is.

The alchemy of practice depends upon our strategic and simultaneous use of all the postures. When arranged rightly, they converge upon us in a way that pressurizes us with a rare and singular force, and we find ourselves at the effect of a more and more direct reality. Even though from an external viewpoint an outside observer would see no more than an unbroken continuity of ordinary activity, our simultaneous and intentional participation in those activities favors the extraordinary circumstance that is required for transformation.

If we permit the resulting pressure to build beyond the habitual point at which we usually panic from feeling so alive, we will graduate into a world of paradoxes, exceptions and mysteries that do not satisfy our preconceived notions of how things should be. This is experienced as a profound creative tension that can build to such a level that the very human attachments, identifications and psychological manifestations we took to be obstacles are suddenly transmuted into the diamond of presence; exactly the way coal, surrounded by nothing more than dirt and stone, becomes a diamond as a result of ordinary matter exerting itself upon the coal with extraordinary force.

This can only occur, however, when we become spectacularly free of distraction and all other types of attention-devouring pests which usually feed upon us without interruption, and by sustaining the accumulated force of our attention without that pressure leaking out of a weak point in our posture.

In North America, these distractions, leak points and preoccupations are so rampant, and so socially sanctioned by our culture, that honoring the lifestyle postures is a very arduous challenge. Why just be with ourselves as we are in reality when we can be surfing on the Internet and enjoying "virtual reality"? Why confront the truth of our emotional lives when we can be sipping a super-sized, triple-shot mocha latte on practically any street corner in the universe?

We have movies, videos, the stock market, new cars, fast and fancy foods, clothing stores, gadget stores, and appliance stores. (Who are you anyway if you can't juice your fruits and vegetables on at least as many speeds as you have cable channels?) We can communicate instantly with anyone anywhere in the world by car phone, cell phone, mobile phone, fax, e-mail, or Internet phone, engaging in endless conversations through which we can solidify our current point of view.

We can take classes morning, noon and night and earn degrees upon degrees that will ensure we're overqualified for most available jobs. A few master's degrees and at least one Ph.D. are better than having to face ourselves and an Md.S. (Minor Degree of Suffering) any day. And hey, let's not hog all the extracurricular activity for ourselves; let's get our kids on the bandwagon. They can go to swimming class, gymnastics, skating, hockey, soccer, football, basketball, science club, nature camp and play group. While we're driving them back and forth we can learn languages on cassette or listen to health specialists and get home repair advice on talk shows.

If we're feeling a little off, no need to introspect, we can just call our doctor, nutritional consultant, therapist, neurolinguistic programmer, astrologer, chiropractor, physiotherapist, surgeon, naturopath, homeopath, psychopath, or a family member. And in some instances we can cover those last two with just one phone call.

Not only can our lives be this packed with excitement, achievement and activity, but we can capture it all with photos, video and audio recordings. Who cares that we weren't even there in the first place, when we can remember how removed we were from the present moment again and again? We can show our kids pictures of them when they were children. "Look, sweetheart, here's another picture that Daddy took standing way back away from you with a big piece of expensive photographic equipment right in between us." Yes, and make those recordings in digital format so they can be fired across the world via the World Wide Web and downloaded into the homes of people you've never met and who couldn't care less.

At least there's still the sanctuary of sleep. But wait. You don't have to waste even that time anymore. You can play your choice of ocean wave music with empowering subliminal messages. Become a sexy millionaire and earn a degree in law while you slumber. Oh yes, what a wonderful world we do live in.

Yet, as wonderful as it is, this world is not content without your dollar in its pocket. As a result, these influences are not happy to float in the background of culture hoping someone will come along and seek them out. We have to make sincere and vigilant efforts to avoid succumbing to the plethora of distraction options that abound. A local cable company in my own city once sent its entire subscriber population an advance bill for a channel package upgrade with the instruction that each household should contact them if they *didn't* want what was being offered. Fortunately, this created a massive revolt on the part of their buying public. (We canceled our cable altogether, never to reconnect). But this reverse billing process is occurring in more ways than we think, only more subtly at the level of our attention.

This is why the practice of formal sitting or the practice of presence alone is unlikely to make any headway. Even if the revelatory nature of true presence were actually glimpsed, without the supporting practices such an opening is about as likely to endure as would a single pancake at a breakfast buffet.

To practice these postures becomes a means by which we can, to put it in the words of Gurdjieff, "build a soul." Gurdjieff's provocative argument is that we are not born with a soul, but rather must earn one through the heat of practice. Indeed, though he taught over half a century ago, he seemed to know that "soul" was going to be harder and harder to come by.

The following sections will cover some of the core benefits of the lifestyle postures without going into too much depth, since each of these areas could be the subject of an entire book on its own. Let us look at each of them from the standpoint of their benefit to the practice of presence and to the integration of spirit so that we can bring our meditation to life.

Study

There are multiple benefits to study. When the master lute player was asked, "How do you make such beautiful music?" he answered, "It's simple, the strings must be neither too tight, nor too loose." Study can be very much like a pitch pipe or a tuning fork to which we tune our practice, adjust it to an appropriate tension—not too lax, not too rigid. The experiences and examples of others who have practiced long and hard themselves can serve as signposts along the way, helping us to have some sense of direction and to make informed decisions about our movement on the path. As the saying goes, "If you come to a fork in the road, take it." We have to keep moving forward, and study is often invaluable in that respect. Many times it is not even that we get hard and fast data, although sometimes that happens and it's invaluable, but that we catch a glimpse of a mood or attitude that gets inside of us and starts to work an invisible magic which we may not even come to know about until it's fully formed within us and we're suddenly behaving and even feeling differently.

Through study we may learn about shortcuts and even hidden trails that can save us from running into unnecessary trouble. Or study may warn us not to take what looks like a shortcut, but to stick to the middle of the main road. In this way study is like a map.

Even more important, however, than getting a detailed

outline of the lay of the land is getting information about our current location. A perfectly drawn map is of no use in getting us home if we don't know from where we're beginning within that schema. Study serves this purpose. Descriptions of phases, states and obstacles help us to consider the reality of our *current* condition and gain clarity about that condition. From there we can move forward with confidence, using our map to guide us as we go.

More than just letting us glean new information, study often reminds us what we already know and perhaps need to own more fully by taking appropriate action in our lives. Sometimes good fiction can be just as valuable as straight spiritual teachings, especially if through those stories we meet characters who are richly developed and show us the weaknesses and strengths of human nature. We can be inspired by such characters to acquire or avoid those strengths and weaknesses.

My own teacher often recommends biographies for his students to read. Real life stories of individuals who have succeeded in the mastery of some art or skill can be tremendously valuable. Such real life examples always bear out the irreplaceable need for discipline and intention in the mastery of any skill or in any field of endeavor.

In addition to this type of literature, there is a vast world of resource material that deals directly with the spiritual path and with spiritual practice. Literature, poetry, philosophical works and psychology, all are relevant to a life of wisdom and successful practice. We want to borrow as much experience as we can, since everything we read has the potential of providing us with some small key that will prove invaluable later. We want to borrow and borrow widely. As the late playwright and author Wilson Mizner reminds us, "If you steal from one, it's plagiarism; if you steal from many, it's research."

Wherever we stand on the path, we can find written material that perfectly addresses our position. When we begin to relinquish our grip on a life of separation, anxiety and the focus of achievement and material gain, we may feel lost and even crazy in comparison to the machine of Western culture which is speeding to nowhere around us. Spiritual literature can be our way of keeping good company as we read the writings of others who have carved a path for themselves through the thicket of the conventional world. Our aims can be supported and nurtured by the right study material. I have often felt as though my hand was literally being held and I was being guided past many pitfalls and through times of discouragement by writers and spiritual practitioners who took the trouble to record their experiences.

While experiences of union and grace, or of separation and pain, are viscerally felt and require no intermediate translator to explain, justify or interpret, the way we integrate these experiences into our daily lives is going to depend on our context. Without education, we could use our spiritual experience to make extreme assumptions about our place in the world. We could interpret our pain as being a creation of our environment or circumstance or due to a flaw in our character instead of understanding that it is arising predictably and lawfully from engaging an inner process. Without education and the examples provided by others, we are more susceptible to delusions of grandeur or illusions of worthlessness; we become a messiah or a *schmuck* instead of an ordinary person who is growing into a true human being.

In order for you to live humorously and intelligently . . . education is needed. The more you study about God and the laws of this Work, clarifying your own confusions, and confirming your own experience through Traditions, the more likely it will be that you are laying the foundation for living a life perfectly aligned with the Will of God.

When one is rightly educated, one finds it easier to accept one's natural state of being. When one is not rightly educated, and that one experiences his or her natural state of being, he or she usually freaks out, terrified of the intensity and vastness of their perceptions.

When one is educated properly, it is more likely that one can deal with experience as it arises very simply and spontaneously, with joy. When one is not educated properly, one typically gets depressed or elated when different experiences arise. Either way, high or low, it doesn't matter for either response is a reaction, rather than a natural acceptance of "what is."[1]

Study helps us to approach our practice with understanding, maturity and strength rather than with a blind faith or unrealistic expectations. This is especially true if we are working with a flesh and blood spiritual master. There are many examples of study material that give us a tremendous amount of support if we are in mid-process with a teacher. We can study the example of other student-teacher relationships and use those examples to keep our head above water as we struggle to make best use of our guide.

Exercise

If we manage to bring ourselves into the present moment, we're going to find ourselves in a human body. Wherever you go, there's your body. If this isn't true in your own case, you've come to the wrong planet, since the game here on planet earth, as far as spiritual work goes, is human incarnation and physical embodiment. Exercise may not be the easiest thing for us to do, but we might as well like the body we're living in, and exercise can go a long way in that department. If our body is not well-tuned, if it feels unhealthy and uneasy, we're not going to have much incentive to *want* to be in the present moment.

We often tend to look at the mind as a separate entity from the body itself, yet every day there is more and more evidence demonstrating their interdependency. Simply at the level of physiology, to move and exercise the body regularly is to stabilize a body chemistry that can stabilize the mind.

For example, the stress response that is mediated by the sympathetic nervous system releases the hormones of adrenaline and cortisol into the bloodstream when an individual is subject to stress. When we encounter events that are potentially life threatening, these hormones flood the bloodstream, and they in turn trigger the release of glucose and fatty acids, which are the fuels that muscles use to contract. This entire chemical sequence is part of the "flight or fight" response. This is certainly appropriate if we are about to be eaten by a tiger. We appropriately run, and if we get away the glucose and fatty acids coursing through the body get burned up in the process and we reenter a balanced resting state. If the tiger catches us, on the other hand, it takes one bite and says, "Oh, man, this guy is full of chemicals. I need to start eating organic."

As we discussed in an earlier chapter, however, we are prone to *interpret* events as being life-threatening even when "flighting" or "fighting" are not really appropriate to the situation.

Let's say we're in the grocery store, about to lay our hands on the last remaining Baby Ruth bar in the store, and someone else unknowingly cuts us off and tosses it—our absolute favorite candy bar—into their cart. Obviously not a life-threatening situation in actuality, but since ego can't tell the difference between the threat of losing one's actual life and the threat of not getting what it wants in any given instant, the mind reacts exactly the same way and sends the signal to the sympathetic nervous system to initiate the stress response. The hormones and then the glucose and fatty acids flood the circulatory system, heart rate increases, blood vessels constrict and muscles tense, creating an overall tension and agitation in our body. "Flight or fight" describes a physiological condition that is an invitation to action—a condition out of which we often, because we feel agitated and tense already, start looking around for a justifiable target. Like Clint Eastwood, our trigger finger is itching. "Go ahead, make my day" is what this chemistry seems to be saying. Then, if someone obliges by giving us the slightest excuse, we're happy to go off like a two-megaton bomb.

Since we're often at the effect of our minds, which, through generated perceptions, create actual stress, exercise is a great way to reinstate a condition of chemical balance in the body. We don't address the root cause this way, but it's a starting point to achieving the balance from which we *can* address the root cause. So the next time you see someone pushing their shopping cart through the store at 25 mph, you'll know what happened.

The "mind" we have is, in part, a reflection of our overall body-brain chemistry, which is determined by our habits of thinking, our diet, the company we keep, the air we breathe, how much sunlight we get, the type and amount of physical affection we give and receive, and exercise. There are many other factors that can contribute to the stability or volatility of our chemistry, but exercise has a particularly strong voice in this determination and can call the mind to balance in even extreme circumstances. Just as thoughts that arise in the mind can cause physiological reactions in the body, physical movements in the body can activate certain kinds of thoughts and moods and be the anchor for overall well-being. This is the entire basis of practices like tai chi.

Exercise can also reestablish our breathing pattern in a natural rhythm if we've strayed from that state due to emotional, physical or psychic tension. Aerobic exercise increases our capacity to deliver and use oxygen, which is associated with one's ability to hold *prana,* or life force, in the cells of the body.

Our willingness to exercise the body has obvious implications with respect to establishing a strong posture in sitting practice. The posture we carry in work and recreation is as vital to our presence in daily life as the posture we hold in formal sitting is to the depth of our silent meditation period. The posture of the body we strive for in sitting practice is an invocation of neutrality; that neutrality in turn is able to host the spontaneity of creative intelligence. The posture that we endeavor to cultivate in daily life is an invocation of elegance; that elegance in turn represents the balance out of which true responsiveness can arise.

If, for instance, we simply have trouble managing our own body weight getting out of the bathtub, or can't easily get out of the way of oncoming vehicles as a pedestrian crossing traffic, we're going to be burdened by unnecessary apprehension as we move through life. The more capable we are of responding to a variety of physical circumstances, the more we can afford to relax our attention toward survival interests.

Exercise combined with awareness is a fundamental means by which we establish elegance and can educate the body in being able to respond fluently and appropriately in any given life situation. The more highly trained our "moving center" is (a term that Gurdjieff used to describe the instinctual intelligence of the body), the more we will be able to hold presence in relationship to our environment and given circumstance.

Dag Hammarskjöld offered this description of such a person in his book, *Markings.*

> Smiling, sincere, incorruptible—
> His body disciplined and limber.
> A man who had become what he could,
> And was what he was
> Ready at any moment to gather everything
> Into one simple sacrifice.[2]

A disciplined and limber body is attained by apprenticing to some form of training that initiates the body into the capacity for radical responsiveness—radical responsiveness being the kind of attentiveness that is able to take its cues from outside of the framework to which the conventional mind is generally oriented. The conventional mind is always expecting something, and that expectation creates a lack of balance that handicaps our ability to respond. We must be "ready for anything, but expecting nothing," as the Zen maxim states.

To break free from the conventional framework which demands that we think, doubt, vacillate and intellectually decide before we act, and to learn instead to be obedient to the instincts of the natural body, we can seek training in a traditional art form. Japanese culture has been particularly generous in providing methods of training the body through art and movement. Masters of calligraphy, *ikebana* or flower arranging, archery, and martial arts have all taught the fundamental reorientation of attention in and through the body that is required to imbue these art forms with the presence of objective spirit.

Traditional practices such as martial arts, which strengthen the body, are valuable to engage for another reason. Usually they are taught by individuals who themselves have a strong practice. To simply be in the company of the instructor is to receive a teaching about the value of discipline. To witness the example of an individual who has transmuted years of effort into the elegance of practice in form is a very powerful transmission directly to the body itself. In selecting our discipline we would do well to find a teacher whose very presence and bearing inspires us to train and carry ourselves with spontaneity and grace.

If we cannot find a tradition with an unbroken lineage of mastery to which we can apprentice, then our chosen form of exercise should be as simple as possible. Swimming, walking, and cycling are all excellent forms of exercise that bring us into a natural rhythm and harmonize the entire system, both physiologically and psychologically.

Many people have reported "flow" experiences in relationship to sporting activities like tennis, skiing or golf. If we drop the shadow of our "movement editor" and free ourselves to respond in these activities from the wisdom of active presence, we can have amazing peak experiences that can be doorways into operating beyond the ordinary mind. Ken Wilber refers to these as "peek" experiences, which they will continue to be—random moments of revelation—unless we can stabilize ourselves in the practice of all the postures. Many people are thrill seekers, mountain climbers, skydivers and race car drivers for this reason—ever trying to meet the moment in high-risk activities that force them into the present. It is true that exercise as a practice to support presence will not succeed if we permit ourselves to languish in a no-stress situation, but it also doesn't succeed if we overstress the system in pursuit of constant adrenaline rushes that we mistake for religious experience.

Through the principle of presence, we can find these kinds of free moments in pursuits that are not life threatening. When we can be engaged in ordinary activity and be totally in the body, the body automatically begins to function like a sifting screen that gets used in panning for gold. The most inconsequential and valueless material begins to sort itself away from the gold through the activity of exercise. The more we inhabit the moment in the body, especially through natural full-body participation in exercise, the more sifting that gets done, and suddenly things have been naturally prioritized in our attention. Fleeting concerns get separated from heartfelt aims, petty interests fall away to reveal our essential needs.

The forms of exercise we choose for regular fitness should benefit not only the muscles of the body, but also the mood of receptivity, the disposition of aesthetics. Our exercise regimen ought to support our ability to fit in rather than to stand out. We should finish our practice each day with a confidence that arises from our flexibility, not from a certainty that we will be able to dominate. For this reason the practice of aikido would be preferable to karate, and ballet would be better than boxing.

A relationship to an ongoing form of exercise is a tangible way for us to see how practice really works. Exercise clearly shows us that we have to put something on the line, that we have to make actual efforts to get actual results. If we don't put on our walking shoes and go the distance, we don't get the benefit. This is true in all areas of our practice. When it comes to training the mind, the results are not quite as visible and measurable, but success with contextual practice is subject to precisely the same laws, and we need a practice habit that fully acknowledges that fact.

Exercise simply reminds us of the joy that is inherent in human embodiment. Exercise reminds us that nothing else is really needed; the body already knows. We work so hard to educate ourselves and try to hold that education in our minds, even though it keeps slipping through the cracks like a handful of water. The purpose of practice in the body is that our very bodies themselves become educated in the conduct of right life.

If we have a body that is healthy, bright and clear of disease, our ability to turn inward and consider a life of spirit is dramatically improved. The true doorway into the domain of spirit, beyond the body into a trans-body condition, arises naturally from a whole-body relationship to ordinary life. This is quite different from an out-of-body state that arises from a disassociation with human life. If we are not fully present in the body, we cannot hope to dance with the moment.

Diet

Gosh, do we really have to talk about this? Maybe we could talk about something a little less likely to create an argument —like maybe religion or politics.

For many of us, food is so deeply associated with emotional issues that it's very difficult to even *discuss* making changes in our eating habits, much less be able to stick to a simple, vegetarian-based eating plan. Since we often come to depend on certain foods to feel safe through their familiarity, or as a substitute for love, we're ready to drive a well-aimed fork through the heart of anyone who suggests we begin weaning ourselves from food that does not support us from a physical standpoint.

This is mostly because food is a way in which many of us distract, cover up, or steal energy away from what could otherwise be a natural and vibrant life of having *real feelings.* There is a lot of energy in feelings; they are themselves a rich source of fuel on the path. If we keep covering up these feelings, or dedicating the energy that arises from them into digesting fats that are about as soluble as automotive lubricants, we're compromising our energy system. As we discussed earlier, most of us panic when we get too much energy—when we begin accessing more than the amount to which we've become habituated. Completely unconsciously, we use digestion to stunt the growth of our fledgling spirit life by eating the wrong things.

To pay attention to our diet is as much a function of *how much* we eat as it is of *what* we eat. Like filling our gas tank in the car, we can get a full reading on the gauge and a lot of miles out of the machine without having to top it off. Yet some of us are so used to filling up the tank until fuel is gushing back out of the pipe that simply to push away from the table one helping short of overflowing is challenging. An ability to recalibrate our "full" point and reliably avoid exceeding it can alone change the whole dynamic of our energy system. Of course, we can compromise our energy system by undereating as well. Either way—leaning too hard into the table or too far back from it—can inhibit our gaining optimum benefit from food as an energy source.

If, in addition, we start substituting nutrient-dense foods for the empty calorie foods that we've knighted as staples, and we diminish our overall calorie intake while maintaining or increasing the nutritional value of our diet, we've made another big leap in the direction of vitality and energy for presence.

Yes, I did say "vegetarian" earlier, and for mostly one simple reason. The energy required to digest fruits, vegetables, grains, nuts, beans or legumes is far less than what is required to digest pot roast. From a standpoint of simple energy conservation, it's more efficient as well as healthier. The cleaner and easier we burn the fuel we need to get through our day, the better.

So we have energy management at the level of our choice of foods and what it requires of us to digest them. Then we have energy management at the level of how we eat that food. Do we eat it in a hurry? Do we actually chew our food so we get the full advantage of its nutrition? Do we combine it properly for maximum benefit? Do we eat our food in an atmosphere of tension or distraction, in which case the subtle energy or nurturing quality of the food may not be assimilated at all? Do we chronically eat when we're bored, angry, depressed, sorrowful or "horny" without realizing that what we're doing is the equivalent of watering a weed that's going to put a root system even more deeply into our precious energy supply?

Perhaps, in the end, we manage to eat healthily and appropriately for our body type but spend a huge amount of energy between meals just thinking about food, debating about supplements, planning our meals, worrying if we're getting enough protein, browsing through the supermarket, preparing and fussing over our food. Some people just love to cook, which is not what I'm referring to. I'm talking about determining whether the attention we give to food is being monopolized by a neurotically-based preoccupation, because this also can waste our energy.

Even if we're eating a reasonably clean diet—and especially if we're not—we're supplementing our real food diet with a whole heap of emotion-backed demands. If we don't get the right thing, at the right time, and in just the right amount, there's a problem. If our rump isn't roasted facing due east by an apron-wearing baroness who was actually there when Heimlich first maneuvered, we've lost our appetite.

When we eat an appropriate amount of food instead of too much or too little, we are more sensitive to subtle levels of awareness. When we eat healthy and nutritious food, we support our energy system so it can operate with maximum vitality. Finally, if we're not living to eat, but rather eating to live as a general orientation, we will free ourselves psychically and emotionally to dive into our meditation practice and dissolve the emotional barriers that stand between ourselves and the radiance of presence.

Right Livelihood

The straight-up and simple standard for right livelihood is that we find work that does not harm others and, ideally, which serves others with maximum benefit. That's pretty self-explanatory. We don't have to elaborate on the difficulties of attempting to be in the present moment if we're in the habit of pushing drugs at the local school or trying to market nuclear warheads to third world countries. If the work we engage gives us some degree of satisfaction and serves in general as a point of connection and opportunity for cooperation with others, then we're way ahead of the game.

The corollary of this principle is to consider the effect that our work has on us. Are we in a high-stress situation at work that makes it very difficult for us to remain present with ourselves or with others? What kind of company do we keep at our workplace, and if it is not good company, do we have the strength to practice while remaining in that atmosphere or, practically speaking, do we need a more supportive environment while we establish a foundation for our meditation practice? Sometimes we don't have the luxury of choice when it comes to the specifics of our work environment or our work partners. Other times, we ourselves unconsciously seek out stressful circumstances to avoid having to become vulnerable to ourselves and others.

Many of the Eastern traditions that have been the birthing grounds of rich spiritual wisdom have been mimicked in form in the West while being misunderstood in context; we've thrown out the baby and *kept* the bath water. India, for example, is spiritually rich in tradition, but not oriented toward material riches as a culture. The combined result of this circumstance was asceticism—wandering beggars who renounced all possessions as a formal declaration of their dedication to spiritual practice. The relinquishment of possessions was intended to *symbolize* the surrender of personal identity. Yet we in the West imported only the poverty aspect of the ascetic equation and mistook it for the essence of India's spiritual teaching. This alongside Jesus' admonishment that a camel can fit through the eye of a needle sooner than a rich man can get into heaven, and suddenly our entire culture has shackled poverty to the ankles of spirituality and now we are tripping all over ourselves.

One of the fundamental teaching lessons which Indian spiritual master Osho Rajneesh demonstrated consistently was that spirituality and poverty not only are not synonymous but are, in fact, in direct opposition. Rajneesh became famous in America for his collection of Rolex watches and

Rolls Royce cars. Having been a resident myself at the Oregon property while he was active there, I witnessed how adamant he was about wanting to address the insidiousness of the "spirituality equals poverty" equation.

Spiritual practice requires energy. Money and material goods, used skillfully, are valuable resources. In fact, if we wish to make any headway in our practice life, we could do with an abundance mentality in all areas of our lives. The mentality of abundance gives us a foundation on which we can build toward the skillful use of various types of energy assets and toward learning the kind of good husbandry of those resources which will benefit the path. If we're coming from a place of scarcity—financially, emotionally or physically—we have little to work with for practice.

Often those who would be able to engage in spiritual practice are not willing, and those who are willing are not able. By virtue of our fortuitous circumstances in Western culture, many of us have been given the *ability* to practice; we are endowed with the basic education, maturity and earning potential that could support spiritual life. Our willingness depends upon to what extent we're inclined to dedicate those circumstances to this end. What, for instance, do we do with the free time we earn from working hard? Do we waste that time in idle pursuits? Would we be willing to devote our precious vacation time to a meditation retreat or to a four-day workweek that would allow us time for study, exercise, and meditation?

But even if we set aside time for formal practices, or manage to arrange an occasional retreat time, we are not a culture of ascetics. We're not going to last very long going door to door with a begging bowl, eschewing the responsibilities of an ordinary householder so we can meditate day and night. Once again, the name of the game for us in the West is integration.

To integrate the essential value of asceticism is how we get the baby back and let the bath water go. Finding that essential value requires that we make a distinction between actual life-in-a-loincloth renunciation and our *willingness* to renounce anything that compromises our ability to be present in any given moment. Fundamentally, we're speaking about examining our attachments and confronting them with an investigation of our motives and hidden agendas. What are we afraid of losing? What are our material attachments a replacement for?

The reality of our lives at the level of money is very telling of our attitudes about energy, abundance versus scarcity, and success. We can hardly move forward effectively with our spiritual practice if we're harboring deep-seated emotional wounds which demand that we remain in scarcity in order to honor a pact we made with our father when we were three. Maybe we unconsciously agreed to never be more successful than he was. Or perhaps our parents wanted nothing more than our own success at a financial level, yet their neglect of us our emotional needs led us to express our anger by defying their material orientation to the world. On the other hand, we may be so attached to our earning potential and to climbing the corporate ladder that the integrity of our practice life is undermined by our inability to stop accumulating and achieving.

Formal meditation can loosen the psychic harness that keeps us rigidly clinging to an emotionally traumatic past or bound by an addiction to temporary status and impermanent circumstances. Paradoxically, if our inner practice is strong and we address our attachments at the root, we may find that we're called to give up nothing at all at an external level. But we must be *willing* to let go of our obstacles for this to become true. If we commit to the path yet are unwilling to examine these attachments, reality itself often intervenes at an external level to assure the continuity of our process. We can save ourselves a lot of trouble by developing a proactive internal practice.

The heart of asceticism, then, is to find renunciation at a level of open attitude and disidentification, yet not to extend this stance into a justification for withdrawal or a lifestyle that is devoid of energy, resources and worldly participation. In short, we must discover that renunciation is not about having nothing, but about having nothing *to lose*. Once this inner work becomes an established foundation for us, we are then ripe to engage in right livelihood in its true sense.

The late Indian sage Swami Papa Ramdas, in his inimitable way, describes the authentic spirit of renunciation.

> External renunciation of work, in which God has engaged us, is not necessary. No action by itself is sinful. No field of work is undesirable. Our ignorance, the cause of misery, consists in our thinking "I", the individual, as the doer of work. No change of situation can bring us peace and rest unless, simultaneous with the change, the ego-sense of actorship also vanishes away.[3]

Success on the spiritual path, whether we are attempting to generate profit for our own evolution or make progress on the path possible for others, depends upon our ability to shrewdly manage an energy balance sheet. As in business, if we want Spirit Inc. to grow, we have to wisely manage the company's resources, saving where appropriate, spending where appropriate, making the right short- and long-term investments, and acquiring assets.

Right livelihood is one such asset in the successful organization of presence. My teacher recommends to his students that they find work that yields the most amount of money in the least amount of time. Of course, that work has to be legal, and not just legal from the standpoint of legislated law, but legal in the context of spiritual law. If making very good money in a minimal amount of time involves acting with a lack of integrity that deepens our own sense of separation from others; creates mistrust, fear and anger in them; or even takes advantage of others without their knowledge, we are not operating within the legal limits of our practice.

A life of right livelihood can serve as the offering that a dedicated practitioner makes to be a bridge between the needs of evolving consciousness and the resources of the material world. This is the crucial difference between the cultural context of asceticism in the East and the spiritual context of renunciation that is appropriate for us in the West.

It's much like the relationship a hunting dog has with its master. If we have one eye glued to our intention for spiritual practice, then presence becomes the master. We then allow the "dog"—which may be our passion for, skill at, or interest in earning money, developing property, writing, or cooking healthy food—plenty of leash. We allow the dog to hunt and retrieve energy in the form of wealth, beneficial circumstances, networks of individuals, or educational resources, but at the same time we train the dog to bring that which it tracks to the feet of our intention to practice. So the "dog" never keeps and eats these things for itself, but delivers them for us to make best use of them and to integrate them into our lives.

If we borrow the Eastern cultural model of asceticism, we wind up training the hunting instinct out of the dog altogether, training him not to bark or taking him to the vet to be neutered, which doesn't help us renounce or transcend anything in our culture. It only represses our own preestablished cultural drives, which are basically life positive—drives to contribute within the context of our own culture, to evolve and expand ourselves.

On the path we come to view wealth not from the perspective of holdings or portfolios, but as an ability to participate, to give and receive. Wealth then is redefined as a system with a lot of energy flowing through it. When we know how to earn and how to spend and invest wisely, we become responsible for the living process or flow that is actual wealth. The acquisition, nurturing and deployment of energetic resources on behalf of presence is right livelihood.

Monogamous Relationship

In the practice of meditation there is absolutely no contradiction between the arising of sexual energy in the body and presence. The predominance of the Victorian attitude which shames and shuns this force is a great hurdle for Westerners who are laboring under layers of culturally induced neuroses which on one hand encourage the repression of our sexuality and on the other feed an obsession with it.

To get the basic energy needed for meditation practice it is, in fact, essential that the energy of sex be embraced. The only point at which our work is obviated is when we fail to remember the purpose of embracing these energies and take them as the end in and of themselves. This is, unfortunately, all too common. The thrilling sensations which surround thoughts of sex, the delight of its pursuit, and the mighty ability of orgasm to galvanize our attention into the present moment (as brief as that one moment is) all become convincingly worthy of pursuit in their own right.

Of all possible preoccupations, the lure of sex—the biological imperative to procreate—is perhaps the strongest, next to survival itself. It is no wonder that the powerful energies of sexual attraction and sexual union have become such a focus in the advertising, marketing and sale of just about every imaginable product in the Western world. Our fascination with sexual imagery has been brought to an all-time peak, a frenzy of anticipation, relished by the unconscious forces of our psychosexual machinery with a verve that is directly proportional to our lack of presence. These unconscious sexpectations then dominate our attention.

A man goes to see a psychiatrist to address his obsession with pornography. The psychiatrist begins asking him questions and within a few minutes has pulled out the Rorschach Test and is holding up cards one by one.

"What do you see in this ink-blot?" he asks the patient.

"A woman bathing by a stream," the man replies.

"What do you see in this one?" the psychiatrist asks, holding up another card.

"Two women getting undressed," the man answers.

"How about this one?" the therapist continues.

"A woman and a man making love," the patient remarks without hesitation.

"Well," the doctor sighs, "you do seem to have quite a fascination with sexual imagery."

The patient looks at the doctor and says, "Me? You're the one who keeps showing me pictures of naked women."

This unconscious process of creating sex in our minds, with the help, of course, of television commercials, magazine ads, billboards, feature films, news stories and product packaging, drains our energy into craving and desire. This mind-sex is difficult to overcome, and the practice of meditation helps us to buck this habit of unencumbered fantasizing, to return to the actual feelings and sensations which are present in the body, and eventually to reestablish a healthy, present-moment relationship to the primal energy of sex. If at an actual and external level, however, we allow ourselves to play out the fugitive tendencies of our psychology, always granting it permission to flee from intimacy and giving in to the mind's evasion of devoted relationship (with ourselves or with another), it will be extremely difficult for us to make friends with Eros.

Eros, the potent and irresistible god of love and desire, has the power to turn our passion willy-nilly toward any passing trifle, to loop us from brief affair to brief affair. Monogamous relationship is the agreement we make with Eros in which we promise *not to resist* desire and passion. In return, Eros promises not to distract us from the context of practice. The meeting place where this agreement is enacted and honored is monogamy. Monogamy is the crucible in which practice and passion achieve the union that is presence itself.

The core practice of meditation is to be *monomomentus,* a Greek word I made up which means "faithful to one moment"—devotion to life-as-it-is in its present form. If our passion for presence is deep and true, we will find a naturally arising commitment to our current primary relationships, as they are. We will thrill with the idea of leaving our interpretations of the other in the dust and meeting that individual new, and new again. Suzuki Roshi once said that, even after twenty years of marriage, when his wife walked into the room he still experienced not knowing who she was. When we honor the necessity of our attention being rooted in presence, we dedicate ourselves to one moment, to the life we have, to the partner we have. To be monogamous means we recognize that there is only one game in town. That game is depth. Depth is achieved by digging in one place, not by scraping many surfaces.

Promiscuity then becomes not only the latitude we give ourselves to move from partner to partner, but also wildly from thought to thought, from titillating sensation to titillating sensation. All of these indiscretions undermine both the integration of our growing force of presence and our ability to sense subtler currents of energy.

There is a prepackaged romance that is on sale now at participating dealers, but if we don't read the fine print (or learn from our experience), we'll miss the fact that these flights of fancy, like many other products of our culture, have a planned obsolescence. We'll need another new one tomorrow, which also means we're going to need the latest perfume, clothes that are in fashion, the right car, the perfect shave, the matching eye shadow, and off we go without really seeing what has seduced us into the game of seduction itself.

Once we learn the knack of welcoming our sexual passion with the intention of transforming it, we will be actively open to its free flow, neither indulging nor suppressing it. This conscious openness acts like a surfboard, allowing us to ride this energy into presence. If we try to grab the feeling, sensation, or "wave" and indulge it, attach to it and identify with it, we only get pummeled by it, and we drown in a sea of fire, sinking into the anarchy of a passion which has no master.

Meditation allows us to step back into the body and to learn the art of being there when the powerful energy of sex awakens and is looking for a partner. If we are unconscious in that moment, we pair our own innocent passion with the boarding house roomers of our unconscious who took up residence straight out of a television commercial we once saw or out of the marketing think tank of Calvin Klein. Suddenly our invaluable life force is wandering with a stranger in a field of dreams. If our intention to practice is attendant to the moment of sexual energy's arising, we can take it passionately by the hand and consummate the alchemy of practice. We can harvest the thrill of passion at its source and transmute it into a radiance of presence in life.

CHAPTER ELEVEN

The Education of the Body

Benediction: Faster Than a Speeding Mind

The lifestyle conditions are all for the purpose of educating our very body to rest in a disposition of presence, wisdom and elegance. The jewels of presence, however, have been stolen and enshrined in our preoccupations with money, food and sex. Instead of interacting with these forces as they are, from a foundation of conscious activity, we are seduced into the anguish of unchecked fantasy, desire and fixation. The wealth we enjoy is not here and now, but in a projected kingdom of excess; the food we crave is never in our mouths, but always on our minds; the sex we desire is not satisfied in our own bed, but in an imaginary bordello full of new partners.

If we want the body itself to preside in life—bright, clear and true—we must practice. Each of the three postures discussed earlier in this chapter—the posture of the body, the posture of the mind, and the posture of lifestyle—are inter-dependent codes of conduct. Together they provide the optimal conditions for radical transformation to ignite within us and to be sustained as our ongoing condition.

These practices may seem like a lot of work, and their mere review may trigger our internal resistance to authority. We may feel like it's too much or too hard or that the practices are merely an extension of all the "rules" that were heaped on us in childhood and that shadow us as adults. The practice of presence, however, with its attendant laws and methods, is a rule we obey for only one reason. To bow to the rule of practice allows us to break the one and only rule that is really worth breaking: the rule of separation. We become obedient in form so that we can liberate ourselves in spirit. We enthusiastically comply with practice to sever the constraints of convention, profanity and self-concern.

Most of us, however, are waiting for some divine intervention, waiting for the anvil of motivation to drop on our head so we can really get down to brass tacks. The good news is that *there is divine intervention.* The bad news is that it comes on its own time, unannounced, unexpected. The worse news is that it has already been to visit us—time and time again, even now—and we have turned our back, closed our eyes, buried our head in the sand. Not intentionally, of course, but unknowingly. Practice does not create divine intervention; it only takes advantage of it. Practice creates nothing at all, in fact; it only reveals what is already there. Or we could look at it from Thomas Jefferson's point of view, who simply said, "I'm a great believer in luck and I find the harder I work the more I have of it."

So since we cannot wait until we're practicing to begin practicing, we start from where we are. In the Vietnam War the helicopters that were used in battle were apparently so busy that the mechanics had to do some of the maintenance on them while they were actually in the air. Our own little war is just the same. We don't have the luxury of landing in a "peace" zone, the destination the New Age is always pining after. That peace, if we ever found it, would be the cessation of our privilege to practice. Our very necessity to practice is given to us *because* we have no peace, because as we sit here now we are unprepared, and life is upon us. Life *is* suffering, so practice *is* essential—here and now, on the fly. The more we practice, the less we'll need this kind of book. Then our knowledge will be tacit, unspoken, radiant, and *lived* through us.

Early in his life, Beethoven reportedly engaged in musical competitions in which two competing pianists would take turns offering a basic theme and the other pianist would have to extemporize on it. Beethoven was apparently so prolific in coming up with beautiful variations of these themes that for some time he tried to remember and record those variations. Yet some time later in his career he abandoned trying to remember them because he realized that their source was internal and that he would never run dry of them. The foundation for his ability to channel this profound creative spirit as it expressed itself through music, however, was built through countless hours of training his body at the keyboard, until the body itself was educated beyond the point of having to consider what to do from the viewpoint of remembered expertise.

The point of practice is to become a reliable representative of creative intelligence such that one serves the greater evolutionary needs of life itself. Even if we can open internally and become vulnerable to what it is that evolution wants, we cannot hope to share it unless the body is trained well enough that it can represent that creative intelligence in *form*, through action, gesture, speech and creative expression. This is what practice is for. Anyone is qualified to know God, but few do the work required to be able to play his music.

If we want to play God's music, our spiritual education, like Beethoven's training, must be at our fingertips. We have to trade our knowledgeable intellect for intelligent hands, our sharp analysis for a refined ear. Our education should abide organically in the body instead of cluttering the mind. When this is true of us, then the mind is free to host innocence, to function as conduit—a pure and open channel to the creative intelligence of evolution itself.

Lee Lozowick has said that just as the hand is quicker than the eye, so is benediction faster than the mind. This is why the body itself has to be trained in spiritual practice. If we only train the mind, we'll find ourselves missing the magic. The mind can access endless amounts of knowledge, but only the body can give us wisdom in the moment.

We're trying to make a prison break from our illusions, but the walls are solid constructs of the intellect, and seem impenetrable. Thankfully, we have the body, which is like the dirt floor of this cell. The body is softer than the mind, not so impervious. The supporting practices are digging tools that we use to get into the body. Down and through the body we find a way out of this prison. We don't have to knock down the walls of our illusions; we simply bypass them by going directly down into the body.

We educate the body so that when the moment of opening is at hand we're not scrambling to "understand" and can take the leap without hesitation. If we are only educated in the mind, then we are still in the jail of our beliefs.

Then we're like an ostrich in its cell that cranes its neck forward, passes only its head out between the bars, and starts shouting, "I'm free, I'm free!" We look quite ridiculous to everyone else, who can plainly see that our body, untrained, is still well imprisoned.

In the movie *The Marathon Man*, there is a scene between the protagonist, played by Dustin Hoffman, and the antagonist, played by Laurence Olivier, in which Dustin Hoffman is being tortured in a dentist chair. The script called for Hoffman's character to be exhausted and sleep deprived, starving, unwashed, and ragged with terror. Hoffman apparently worked to ready himself for this scene by actually not sleeping, washing or eating for some significant period prior to the filming and then running around the block just before the first take of the scene. Olivier reportedly remarked to him, "My dear boy, wouldn't it be easier to just act?"

If our training is in our body, we can call upon it at will. If it's in the body, then it isn't acting anymore, it's the real thing, and we're not required to go through a series of mental gymnastics to try and mimic a condition of authenticity. If the body is trained, we don't have to fake it anymore. So we literally have to "exercise" our right to remain silent. Without practice, we have no means to express the muse of silence.

The mind always makes things much more complicated than they need to be. If we want a relationship to the spiritual, we only need to engage the training that is relevant to presence by practicing, and leave the rest alone. Werner Erhard was fond of a demonstration in which he would take a piece of chalk, hold it between his fingers several feet off the floor, and let it fall. He would then proceed to point out that the chalk "has already hit the floor" in the instant that it is released, because gravity and the principles of physics are reliable. Our practice is exactly the same. If we're impeccable in relationship to the postures, we can completely relinquish our attachment to results because the laws of spiritual practice are equally stable, constant and unfailing; it's just a matter of time. The benefit has already occurred. Our "enlightenment" has already hit the floor.

It's a great relief to train properly because then we know what *not* to do. The mind wants things complicated. But in our mind's dedication to *complications,* our attention is held hostage on the surface of reality, we only see the appearances of things, and we entirely miss the *intricacy* of life-as-it-is, which has depth, meaning and richness. Not that practice is easy. Without question it requires of us tremendous efforts—efforts we're going to have to make not just once, but again and again, since, as M. H. Alderson said, "If at first you don't succeed, you are running about average."

The Body Transparent

The alchemy of practice is the clarification of the body and mind as a window to reality. To practice through to this point of clarification is not to reveal the meaning or purpose of the body and mind, but to transcend experience, self-reflection, and "self-understanding" to the no-meaning of life-as-it-is. This clarification is only revelatory in that it reveals that which is beyond the need for meaning and understanding. If the alchemy of practice is not realized, then we are left with some form of fixation on our own reflection—a reflection which is only possible if the body and mind remains opaque and uninvestigated at the level of appearances.

To become "spiritual," "holy," or "conscious" at a level which satisfies our search for an acceptable identity is to miss our opportunity for practice. A little boy said to his

mother, "Mommy, I want to be a musician when I grow up."
His mother looked at him and replied, "Oh, honey, don't
be silly. You can't do *both*." We cannot love the truth if we
are also trying to be the one who "knows" it. The two are
mutually exclusive.

If the alchemy of our practice is complete, it is ongoing.
If there is true clarity, then that clarity has infinite depth.
Such clarity does not allow the luxury of a final resting
point at which the anchor of identity hits bottom and
latches on to the illusion of certainty.

The Wild Heart
of Silence

CHAPTER TWELVE

A Very Sharp Cookie

We have barely addressed the function of the teacher or guru in meditation practice, even though I believe it to be the single most significant factor in determining its success. My teacher has said, "Listen. I'll let you in on a little secret. A path is only as good as its teacher and the willingness of the student to work. The technique is secondary." The fact that I haven't dedicated more of this book to the necessity of the student-teacher relationship is not indicative of its importance or lack of importance. It is, rather, indicative of the foundational work we need to do in general before we can really take full advantage of such a relationship. Yet it simply wouldn't be fair warning, having talked so freely about the practice of meditation, not to discuss two possible consequences of seeking the truth. If one throws oneself with abandon into the brilliance of practice, there are two accidents that are waiting to happen. The first is the appearance of the spiritual master; the second is the disappearance of your self. The arrival of the teacher in our lives, or the departure of our self as we've known it all along, comes not without a sudden disorientation. In either case, we usually experience this circumstance as being fiercely contrary to our old point of view. Since this is often a threatening occurrence, we may question the validity or "sanity" of the teacher or of our own profoundly altered perception, even though it may be our old point of view and the rest of the world which are misguided and in need of being righted in relationship to the true bearing of the human spirit.

The spiritual master represents the inviolable condition of uprightness from which deviation is impossible. This, of course, makes such a person a deviant in the eyes of the common world. He or she who will not deviate into the life scripts of excess, denial and comfort by which most of us navigate our interactions and activities is uncontrollable, wild with heart, crazy with freedom.

Once, while traveling on a long transatlantic flight, Lee Lozowick politely but repeatedly turned down the meals that were being offered on board. The flight attendant became concerned; after all, that's what people are supposed to do on long flights: eat, read, eat, watch movies and . . . eat. After more than ten hours the attendant was practically begging Lee to have something, such was his own discomfort at the idea of going that long without food. My teacher again graciously declined. As the flight attendant walked away Lee quietly commented, to no one in particular, "I eat my mind."

When we come into contact with such an individual, if we are not willing to let our whole world be turned upside-down we are thrown into confusion and turmoil—and, with rare exception, we resist. But I tread on dangerous territory here, broaching such a subject in "modern" times and on Western soil. Our mistrust of authority and our experiences of betrayal, which are both personal and ancestral, collected over generations, are deep and grave. And we have good reason to be suspicious of charlatans, since there are many.

Eventually, however, we have to leave kindergarten; and on the spiritual path you *get* a teacher when you leave kindergarten, whereas in the world, growing up is supposed to be about *not* having to have a teacher anymore. Our world is about becoming your own authority, doing it yourself, being your own expert.

So we flock to teachers who throw us such assurances as, "I'm not a guru; you're your own guide; just follow your heart," and other such consolations that we gobble up like candy. That candy, however, is filled with the lead shot of suffering. We don't see that the reason we've hit bottom is because we're clinging to an anchor, not a life preserver. The anchor is encrusted with the culturally popular gemstones of "independence," "individuality," and "self-knowledge," but it's all costume jewelry so it does not enrich our presence. We wallow in our confusion but have the required amount of denial to be able, in the midst of that turmoil, to defend our "freedom"—our right to create more suffering for ourselves and others in our own unique way.

One day, however, we must make a leap—a leap into the heart of the unknown. And that leap should be made with the educated body we've already discussed, not blindly, not in a desperate seeking for approval and acknowledgement, or even love. But leap we must if we wish to cross into the wild land of silence; into the full quiet of presence. Not only must we leap, but we must be strong and resourceful enough to live in the wild territory of heart, in the jungles of paradox which are the habitat of awakened consciousness.

One of Chögyam Trungpa Rinpoche's personal attendants reports that Trungpa Rinpoche was so committed to his students' development that he regularly threw himself down flights of stairs, forcing those who were with him to be present —ready for anything—risking his own safety to provide the necessity for his students to remain alert. We're obviously not talking about ordinary individuals here. In fact, since such teachers are few and far between we may wonder, how can I attract the help of one?

There is a saying that "the teacher finds us when we are ready." That readiness is advertised by reliable practice. As the owner of a small business, I was told by a marketing consultant that I should consider only the long-term and consistent placement of ads in carefully chosen publications. Practice is where we advertise for a teacher. We place our ads in the same place, over and over, and eventually, by being consistent, we are noticed. If we show up on the meditation cushion again and again, we're drawing the attention of real help.

Practice prepares us because a true master will ask us to stand on our human maturity, discipline and discretion while we're reaching for the heart of surrender. Practice prepares us because every real teacher is praying for a few mature students—students who have a strong enough ego to withstand the mystery of "beginner's mind."[1] Beginner's mind is out of the question if one is working with a beginner's ego. Beginner's ego is represented by one solidified point of view that is defended at all costs. Beginner's mind is the complete openness to *all* points of view at the same time. Such a view requires, first, a breadth of education and experience and, second, enough maturity to abandon identification with rigidified perspectives without dismissing those perspectives altogether.

Many of us cannot conceive of what it would be like to rest wholly in beginner's mind. What would that look like? What would such a person act like? The result of an absence of role models is that Westerners are making it up or turning to the only role models they can find. But to simply be in the presence of a human who has fired the purity of consciousness into the living reality of a daily life is very dangerous, because through such contact we might begin to actually *feel* the immensity of presence, experience the heartbreaking vulnerability of spirit, catch a scent of the perfume of true elegance and grace through its living demonstration by a master. Once that happens, our old lives are put into jeopardy by the call of our own heart.

A friend of mine has a teacher who told him that his work should become his pleasure; his work being his practice. So if we come to the path and we hear the teaching and we start embracing the postures, we've got a big chunk of chocolate trouble on our hands. Once our practice becomes our pleasure, it's addictive. And when we hold that chocolate in our hands long enough, it melts, and underneath all that sweetness is a very sharp cookie, whom we call the spiritual master.

So that's the first accident that's waiting to happen.

CHAPTER THIRTEEN

"Look, Ma, No I"

The second accident is what we might call an experience of "awakening," or shift of context, which involves the sudden loss of identity such as we have previously believed ourselves to possess—identity as a limited, definable person. As Richard Baker Roshi put it, "Enlightenment is an accident. Meditation makes you accident prone."[1]

Remember what it was like when you learned to ride a two-wheeler for the first time? There was something about the discovery that a thing which is essentially precarious and unstable—a bike with two wheels—could become not only stable, but dynamically active in its reliability, once the knack of keeping it in motion was mastered. Then that which was nothing more than a hunk of metal prone to remain on its side became a marvel of movement, even a symbol of freedom.

Remember then, some years later, when you discovered the same delight all over again in the realization that you could let go of the handlebars, relinquish the need to steer, and the bike would *still* remain vertical? The discovery that you could *take away the one you thought had to steer* was then the root of the thrill.

Such is the nature of the discovery of no "I." The first glimpse is likely to arrive like this. By some combination of daring and accident, we let go of the handlebars and find, to our utter surprise, that the stability of our whole apparatus is not dependent on our "being there" in the sense of directing things, hanging on with white knuckles to keep the whole shebang from crashing into a ditch. In fact, we discover that the "I," or the mechanism which does the steering, always keeps us not only on the road, but on the same old road. When this mechanism lets go of the front wheel, suddenly we find ourselves on new paths, enjoying scenic routes, or discovering alternate journeys which offer rewards and evolutionary possibilities we would never have encountered with our old riding habits. So the bike carries on even though "we" are no longer steering; there is just the wonder of the whole upright arrangement as the world and life go by.

Our first impulse is to share our discovery with somebody: the thrill of letting go, the delight of breaking laws we had taken as the unalterable constraints of "reality." In such a moment we want the world to know not what we have accomplished, but what is possible, and to witness the torrent of freedom that floods from surrender. So don't be surprised if you find yourself one day careening by in the ecstasy of having let completely go, two free hands waving madly in the air, calling out, "Look, Ma, no 'I'!"

This shift of context is sudden and uncompromising. Where, when and how it occurs is completely unpredictable. We cannot bring it on or lure it in. Even though, paradoxically, this shift seems to follow on the heels of effort, we cannot look back and declare that our efforts "caused" it, since at that point we are having difficulty reconstituting our sense of being anyone at all.

If we are motivated to practice by the hope that we will break through our self-centered misery and reach "enlightenment," "peace," or some other such destination, we are still goal-oriented. This orientation toward a goal in our life of practice is a very difficult habit to break. It is a sudden shift of context which brings all our efforts down in one breathtaking moment of collapse, and we get a view of our situation that changes our perspective forever.

A young disciple who was training in archery with a master in Japan had become very proficient in not only his accuracy, but in the practice of following his master's instruction in form. One day, as he drew an arrow, the master asked him to wait for his command to release it.

Holding the arrow drawn and ready, the disciple was steady as a statue. In the same instant that the master gave the signal for the disciple to loose the arrow, the master suddenly reached out and grabbed the arrow firmly with his hand. As the young man let the arrow go, the harnessed force in the disciple's deeply drawn bow threw him and his bow backwards *off* the arrow, while the master held it fixed in place.

The disciple looked up from the ground and saw the master holding the arrow by itself in mid-air. In that moment he realized the true meaning of the master's teaching. He saw that there was only the arrow, only the practice of shooting, but no *him*. Who he thought he had always been had been thrown clear of attachment to the form of the practice and to his own form as well. For the first time he came to know the profound silence of pure being.

The master walked over to the disciple, smiled, broke the arrow in the middle, and handed it to him.

This story tells us about the path of the meditator. First we use discipline and attention to true our posture and to refine our form. That effort is like the disciple's bow, fully drawn, a powerful force that we gather with clear purpose and developed skill. If the disciple takes responsibility for this aspect of practice, then, in the right moment, a genuine master can use the strength and maturity of our formal practice to throw us clear of ourselves—into the well of silence and freedom which is our birthright.

Endnotes

Chapter 1: A Guide for the West of Us

1. Todd Stein, "Zen Sells," *Shambhala Sun* 8 (November 1999), 38.
2. Ken Wilber, *A Brief History of Everything* (Boston: Shambhala, 1996), 140.

Chapter 2: The Art of Staying Home

1. Shunryu Suzuki, *Zen Mind, Beginner's Mind* (N.Y.: Weatherhill, 1970), 38.

Chapter 3: There Is No Good Reason to Meditate

1. Suzuki Roshi, quoted in Mariana Caplan, *Halfway Up the Mountain* (Prescott, Ariz.: Hohm Press, 1999), 1.
2. Lee Lozowick, *Beyond Release* (Tabor, N.J.: Hohm, 1975), 92.

Chapter 4: You Had to Be There

1. Ken Wilber, *A Brief History of Everything* (Boston: Shambhala, 1996), 197.
2. Wilber, 198.

Chapter 5: What Do We Have in Mind?

1. Swami Papa Ramdas, *Letters of Swami Ramdas: Volume 1* (Kerala, India: Anandashram, 1982; distributed in North America by The Blue Dove Foundation, www. blue dove.com), 145–146.

Chapter 7: A Delicate Balance

1. Regina Sara Ryan, *Praying Dangerously: Radical Reliance on God* (Prescott, Ariz.: Hohm Press, 2001), 48.

Chapter 8: Sitting Practice: The Posture of the Body

1. Shunryu Suzuki, *Zen Mind, Beginner's Mind* (N.Y.: Weatherhill, 1970), 26.
2. Suzuki, 28.
3. Suzuki, 27.
4. Suzuki, 41.
5. Taisen Deshimaru, *SIT: Zen Teachings of Master Taisen Deshimaru*, ed. Philippe Coupey (Prescott, Ariz.: Hohm Press, 1996), 212.
6. Osho Rajneesh, *Meditation: The Art of Ecstasy*, ed. Ma Satya Bharti (N.Y.: Harper & Row, 1976), 37.
7. Deshimaru, 93.

Chapter 10: Supporting Practices: The Posture of Lifestyle

1. Lee Lozowick, *In the Fire* (Nevada City, Calif.: I.D.H.H.B.; Tabor, N.J.: Hohm Press, 1978), 69.
2. Dag Hammarskjöld, *Markings* (N.Y.: Alfred A. Knopf, 1965), 6.
3. Swami Papa Ramdas, *Letters of Swami Ramdas: Volume 1* (Kerala, India: Anandashram, 1982; distributed in

North America by The Blue Dove Foundation, www.bluedove.com), 28.

Chapter 12: A Very Sharp Cookie

1. The phrase "beginner's mind" is discussed at length in the book: *Zen Mind, Beginner's Mind* (N.Y.: Weatherhill, 1970), by Shunryu Suzuki.

Chapter 13: "Look, Ma, No 'I'"

1. Baker Roshi quoted in Ken Wilber, "Integral Transformative Practice: In This World or Out of It?" *What Is Enlightenment?* 18, Fall/Winter 2000, 37.

Index

156

Additional Titles of Interest
HOHM PRESS

THE PERFECTION OF NOTHING
Reflections on Spiritual Practice
by Rick Lewis

With remarkable clarity, reminiscent of the early writing of J. Krishnamurti or Alan Watts, Rick Lewis weaves practical considerations about spiritual life with profound mystical understanding. Whether describing the "illusion of unworthiness" that most of us suffer, the challenges of spiritual practice, or his own awe in discovering the majesty of the present moment, this book is full of laser-sharp analogies that make complex philosophical/religious ideas attractive and easy to understand. His nonsectarian approach will be appreciated by seekers and practitioners of any religious tradition—whether they are actively engaged in spiritual work, or approaching it for the first time. His words provide guidance and inspiration for revealing the spiritual in everyday life.

Paper, 180 pages, $14.95
ISBN: 1-890772-02-X

THE ALCHEMY OF TRANSFORMATION
by Lee Lozowick
Foreword by Claudio Naranjo, M.D.

A concise and straightforward overview of the principles of spiritual life as developed and taught by Lee Lozowick for the past twenty years. Subjects of use to seekers and serious students of any spiritual tradition include: A radical, elegant and irreverent approach to the possibility of change from ego-centeredness to God-centeredness—the ultimate human transformation.

Paper, 192 pages, $14.95
ISBN: 0-934252-62-9

Visit our website at www.hohmpress.com

ZEN TRASH
Irreverent and Sacred Teaching Stories of Lee Lozowick
Edited by Sylvan Incao

This book contains dozens of teaching stories from many world religious traditions including Zen, Christianity, Tibetan Buddhism, Sufism and Hinduism—rendered with a twist of humor, irony or provocation by contemporary spiritual teacher Lee Lozowick. They are compiled from twenty-five years of Lozowick's talks and seminars in the U.S., Canada, Europe, Mexico and India. Even if they derive from a three-thousand-year-old tradition, Lozowick's unique style makes these stories contemporary and practical.

Paper, 156 pages, $12. 95
ISBN: 1-890772-21-6

HALFWAY UP THE MOUNTAIN
The Error of Premature Claims to Enlightenment
by Mariana Caplan
Foreword by Fleet Maull

Dozens of first-hand interviews with students, respected spiritual teachers and masters, together with broad research are synthesized here to assist readers in avoiding the pitfalls of the spiritual path. Topics include: mistaking mystical experience for enlightenment; ego inflation, power and corruption among spiritual leaders; the question of the need for a teacher; disillusionment on the path . . . and much more.

"Caplan's illuminating book . . . urges seekers to pay the price of traveling the hard road to true enlightenment."
—**Publisher's Weekly**

Paper, 600 pages, $21.95
ISBN: 0-934252-91-2

AS IT IS
A Year on the Road with a Tantric Teacher
by M. Young

A first-hand account of a one-year journey around the world in the company of tantric teacher Lee Lozowick. This book catalogues the trials and wonders of day-to-day interactions between a teacher and his students, and presents a broad range of his teachings given in seminars from San Francisco, California to Rishikesh, India. *As It Is* considers the core principles of tantra, including non-duality, compassion (the Bodhisattva ideal), service to others, and transformation within daily life. Written as a narrative, this captivating book will appeal to practitioners of any spiritual path. Readers interested in a life of clarity, genuine creativity, wisdom and harmony will find this an invaluable resource.

Paper, 840 pages, 24 b&w photos, $29.95
ISBN: 0-934252-99-8

THE JUMP INTO LIFE
Moving Beyond Fear
by Arnaud Desjardins
Foreword by Richard Moss, M.D.

"Say Yes to life," the author continually invites in this welcome guidebook to the spiritual path. For anyone who has ever felt oppressed by the life-negative seriousness of religion, this book is a timely antidote. In language that translates the complex to the obvious, Desjardins applies his simple teaching of happiness and gratitude to a broad range of weighty topics, including sexuality and intimate relationships, structuring an "inner life," the relief of suffering, and overcoming fear.

Paper, 278 pages, $12.95
ISBN: 0-934252-42-4

Visit our website at www.hohmpress.com

SIT: Zen Teachings of Master Taisen Deshimaru
Edited by Philippe Coupey

Like spending a month in retreat with a great Zen master. SIT addresses the practice of meditation for both beginners and long-time students of Zen. Deshimaru's powerful and insightful approach is particularly suited to those who desire an experience of the rigorous Soto tradition in a form that is accessible to Westerners.

"To understand oneself is to understand the universe."

—**Master Taisen Deshimaru**

Paper, 375 pages, 18 photographs, $19.95
ISBN: 0-934252-61-0

THE SHADOW ON THE PATH
Clearing the Psychological Blocks to Spiritual Development
by V.J. Fedorschak
Foreword by Claudio Naranjo, M.D.

Tracing the development of the human psychological shadow from Freud to the present, this readable analysis presents five contemporary approaches to spiritual psychotherapy for those who find themselves needing help on the spiritual path. Offers insight into the phenomenon of denial and projection.

Topics include: the shadow in the work notable therapists; the principles of inner spiritual development in the major world religions; examples of the disowned shadow in contemporary religious movements; and case studies of clients in spiritual groups who have worked with their shadow issues.

Paper, 300 pages, $17.95
ISBN: 0-934252-81-5

THE ONLY GRACE IS LOVING GOD
by Lee Lozowick

Love, God, Loving God, Grace, Divine Will—these subjects have engaged the minds and hearts of theologians throughout the ages, and even caused radical schisms within organized religions. Lee Lozowick dares to address them again, and in a way entirely original. He challenges all conventional definitions of love, and all superficial assumptions about the nature of loving God, and introduces a radical distinction which he calls the "whim of God" to explain why the random and beneficent Grace of loving God is humanity's ultimate possibility. More than just esoteric musings, *The Only Grace is Loving God* is an urgent and practical appeal to every hungry heart.

Paper, 108 pages, $5.95
ISBN: 0-934252-07-6

THE YOGA TRADITION
History, Literature, Philosophy and Practice
by Georg Feuerstein, Ph.D.
Foreword by Ken Wilber

A complete overview of the great Yogic traditions of: Raja-Yoga, Hatha-Yoga, Jnana-Yoga, Bhakti-Yoga, Karma-Yoga, Tantra-Yoga, Kundalini-Yoga, Mantra-Yoga and many other lesser known forms. Includes translations of over twenty famous Yoga treatises, like the *Yoga-Sutra of Patanjali,* and a first-time translation of the *Goraksha Paddhati,* an ancient Hatha Yoga text. Covers all aspects of Hindu, Buddhist, Jaina and Sikh Yoga. A necessary resource for all students and scholars of Yoga.

Paper, 550 pages, more than 200 illustrations, $29.95
ISBN: 1-8990772-18-6

Visit our website at www.hohmpress.com

PRAYING DANGEROUSLY
Radical Reliance on God
by Regina Sara Ryan

Praying Dangerously re-enlivens an age-old tradition of prayer as an expression of radical reliance on God, or non-compromising surrender to Life *as it is*. This approach expands the possibilities of prayer, elevating it beyond ordinary pleas for help, comfort, security and prosperity. *Praying Dangerously* invites a renewal of the inner life, by increasing one's desire to burn away superficial, safe notions of God, holiness, satisfaction and peace.

"A brave book for brave people . . ."

—**David Steindl-Rast,** O.S.B.,
author *Gratefulness, the Heart of Prayer*

". . . wise, fierce, challenging . . ."

—**Andrew Harvey,**
author *The Essential Mystics*

Paper, 240 pages, $14.95
ISBN: 1-8990772-06-2

Retail Order Form
HOHM PRESS

Name _____ Phone _____

Address or P.O. Box _____ _____

City _____ State _____ Zip _____

QTY	TITLE	PRICE	TOTAL
	The Perfection of Nothing	$14.95	
	The Alchemy of Transformation	$14.95	
	Zen Trash	$12.95	
	Halfway Up the Mountain	$21.95	
	As It Is	$29.95	
	The Jump Into Life	$12.95	
	SIT	$19.95	
	The Shadow on the Path	$17.95	
	The Only Grace Is Loving God	$ 5.95	
	The Yoga Tradition	$29.95	
	Praying Dangerously	$14.95	

Surface Shipping Charges   *Subtotal*
1st book or CD $5.00
Each additional item $1.00   *Shipping*

Method of Shipping   TOTAL
_____ Surface U.S. Mail (Priority)
_____ 2nd-Day Air Mail (Mail +$5.00)
_____ FedEx Ground (Mail +$3.00)
_____ Next-Day Air Mail (Mail +$15.00)

Method of Payment
_____ Check or M.O.—Payable to Hohm Press
_____ Call 800.381.2700 to place a credit card order
_____ Call 928.717.1779 to fax a credit card order

Credit Card Information
Card # _____ Exp. Date _____

Visit our website to view our complete catalog!

www.hohmpress.com